PARADIGM CHANGE

THE COLLECTIVE WISDOM OF RECOVERY

A therapist's moving account of her clients' struggles, challenges and triumphs over addiction

L. Georgi DiStefano, LCSW

Published by
Montezuma Publishing
Aztec Shops Ltd.
San Diego State University
San Diego, California 92182-1701
619-594-7552
www.montezumapublishing.com

Copyright © 2017
All Rights Reserved.

ISBN: 978-0-7442-5830-1

Copyright © 2017 by Montezuma Publishing and the author, L. Georgi DiStefano. The compilation, formatting, printing and binding of this work is the exclusive copyright of Montezuma Publishing and the author, L. Georgi DiStefano. All rights reserved. No part of this work may be reproduced, stored in a retrieval system, or transmitted in any form or by any means, including digital, except as may be expressly permitted by the applicable copyright statutes or with written permission of the Publisher or Author.

Publishing Manager: Kim Mazyck
Design and Formatting: Lia Dearborn
Cover Design: Lia Dearborn
Quality Control: Jasmine Baiz

Paradigm Pyramid - Design and Formatting:
Patricia Cabezas Churchill
PDMT Logo: Jeffrey Austin
Author's Photograph: WASIO Photography, San Diego

DEDICATION

TO MY NEPHEW CHRISTOPHER
FOR BRINGING ME GREAT JOY
AND TO MY GRANDDAUGHTERS
MADDY, ANJARA, AND SARAI
FOR THEIR ABUNDANT LOVE AND LAUGHTER

WHAT READERS ARE SAYING ABOUT *PARADIGM CHANGE:*

"Utilizing a case history approach, this book offers a veritable treasury of tools and techniques for successful therapy with the chemically dependent, provided by a proven master in the field!"

Annette R. Smith, PhD., LCSW
Author of *The Social World of Alcoholics Anonymous: How It Works*

"Georgi DiStefano's Paradigm Change – The Collective Wisdom of Recovery is an ideal resource for individual therapy in which she reviews the 12 themes of the Paradigm Developmental model and provides client stories of the challenges faced by individuals in each of the themes. The client stories bring to life how with the help of professional therapy clients can achieve a successful recovery. This is a must read for clients, families, therapists and anyone with an interest in this field."

Janlee Wong,
Executive Director, National Association of Social Workers, California Chapter.

"Everything I learned in nearly 20 years of sobriety and 40 years as a mental health professional, Georgi DiStefano articulates in clear concise fashion in one fabulous text. There is much I didn't know, and learned about the value of varied approaches to Recovery in

addition to AA. Her inclusive acceptance of any proven strategy to achieve progress toward full Recovery in a single book is astounding. Paradigm Change-the Collective Wisdom of Recovery is truly a one-stop shop for a lifetime of recovery treatment wisdom."

    Carole, Los Angeles

"There are many books written about how to get sober, but this book, Paradigm Change: The Collective Wisdom of Recovery is also an excellent tool to use when helping people already well versed in recovery, some with many years of recovery under their belt, but struggling with an unexpected hiccup in their recovery journey."

    Abby Oberg, IMFT, MCA

"After reading Ms. DiStefano's book, I was immensely encouraged to know there are people still out there willing to help people afflicted by addiction. I pray that this well written book gets in to the hands of people who need help and encouragement to lead them on a journey to recovery. As a double winner, I was able to relate to both sides of addiction....and so I believe this book can also help the friends and family of the addicted person."

    Sue, New York
    (30 years of Sobriety)

"In this unique and highly readable book, Georgi DiStefano, LCSW has taken her 40+ years of clinical *practice with clients with substance use disorders, and distilled the themes regarding recovery. She interweaves clients' stories throughout the book, covering important challenges that present in everyday life. DiStefano grounds the book in research as well as lived experience. I highly recommend this book for those that want to learn more about changing drinking or drug use and are looking to live a fuller life."*

    Melinda Hohman, PhD.
    Director and Professor
    North American Associate Editor, *British Journal of Social Work*
    School of Social Work, San Diego State University

One of Georgi's beautiful gifts is her ability to synthesize a lifetime of clinical experience with practical strategies for addressing the myriad of problems associated with substance use disorders. True to form, Georgi has once again made a valuable contribution to the field. Clearly, compassionately, and at times humorously, Georgi offers insights and useful resources that can benefit the layman, paraprofessional, and professional. For those working a program of recovery in the 12-step tradition, this is a wonderful adjunct to the Big Book. For those pursuing an alternative path to recovery, the themes discussed are highly inclusive, respectfully supporting any path one chooses."

    Melanie Barker, MPH, LCSW
    Executive/Clinical Director, SDSU DUIP

THE COLLECTIVE WISDOM OF RECOVERY

"Georgi thank you for this 3rd addition to your series, Paradigm Change-The Collective Wisdom of Recovery. Your generous and incredible contributions to the field of Substance Use Disorder Treatment and Social Work have had a tremendous impact on countless numbers of clients, and what a tremendous resource your work has been and continues to be for providers. I know I am not alone in expressing my respect and gratitude for you and your work. I highly recommend this entire 3 book series."

>Roland Williams, MA, MAC, LAADC, NCACII, CADCII, SAP
>President and CEO, Free Life Enterprises
>Author with Terence Gorski of: *Relapse Prevention for African Americans, Workbook and Textbook*

"Ms. DiStefano has written a wonderful book full of tips and pearls of wisdom for anyone in recovery or struggling with addiction. It is easy to follow and will be of significant assistance in the recovery process. While it is written primarily for those who are experiencing addictive issues in their own lives, psychotherapists can also learn much from this book to help their clients. I recommend this book highly and believe you will find it to be a great addition to your recovery library."

>Jan Parker, PhD, MFT
>Professor, National University San Diego, CA
>Co-Author of *The Clinician's Guide to 12-Step Programs: How, When, and Why to Refer a Client*

Georgi has written a no-nonsense book on ways to assist clients tackle their addictions. This paradigm is an opportunity to help clients who are resistant to traditional addiction models embrace tools to not let their addictions win the battle.

Libby Timmons, M.Ed., LISAC, CEAP, SAP

With Georgi's new book, she offers readers her experience and insight into the change process for both client and clinician.

Gail Donner, CCAPP
Counseling Coordinator, SDSU DUIP

Georgi DiStefano's book, PARADIGM CHANGE: THE COLLECTIVE WISDOM OF RECOVERY, takes away the mystique of alcohol and drug sobriety and opens the reader to the rich culture of change. She includes helpful information on the various types of addiction recovery support groups, resources and the benefits of ongoing psychotherapy. Ms DiStefano offers a rare glimpse into the decisions and routines necessary to navigate this essential paradigm shift for the long term.

Judy Saalinger, PhD., LMFT, CAS
Co-Founder/Executive Director
Lasting Recovery Outpatient Treatment Center

CONTENTS

ACKNOWLEDGEMENTS xvii
FOREWORD xxi
A NOTE TO READERS xxii
INTRODUCTION 1
PROLOGUE - TRANSFORMATION 11
    RAY'S STORY 12
    START WITH THE END IN MIND 16

PARADIGM 1   PROBLEM RECOGNITION 19

CHAPTER 1 - THEME 1
PROBLEM RECOGNITION 21
    "ARE YOU A PICKLE OR ARE YOU A CUCUMBER?" 22
    SCOTT'S STORY 25
    IT TAKES WHAT IT TAKES 27
        CLAUDE'S STORY 27
        DEBORAH'S STORY 29
    A WORD ABOUT TRAUMA 31
    IN SUMMARY 33
    FURTHER INFORMATION 35
        ALCOHOL USE DISORDER - DSM 5 35

CHAPTER 2 - THEME 2
LOOKING BEYOND SELF 39
    INSANITY 40
        BRIAN'S STORY 41

- BREAKING THE VICIOUS CYCLE 43
  - *JEREMY'S STORY* 43
  - *ADIA'S STORY*... 46
  - *A SMART DOCTOR'S STORY*.......................... 47
- ADULT CHILDREN OF ALCOHOLICS 48
- SAPPORO JAPAN... 49
- **FURTHER INFORMATION**................................... 52
  - *MODERATION MANAGEMENT: MM*............... 52

CHAPTER 3 - THEME 3
LETTING GO.. 57
- CHILDREN OF ALCOHOLICS 58
- THE NEGATIVE COMMITTEE 60
- COGNITIVE SCHEMAS 60
  - *SAMANTHA'S STORY*..................................... 62
  - *ESTELLA'S STORY* 65
- CORE BELIEFS... 67
- **FURTHER INFORMATION**................................... 68
- MEDICATIONS FOR TREATMENT OF
  ALCOHOL USE DISORDERS 70
- MEDICATIONS FOR TREATMENT OF
  SUBSTANCE USE DISORDERS 71
- MEDICATIONS FOR NICOTINE USE
  DISORDERS 72
- IN SUMMARY 73

PARADIGM 2   TAKING RESPONSIBILITY 77

CHAPTER 4 - THEME 4
SELF-EXAMINATION 79
THEIR STORIES CONTINUE 82
RAY 82
CLAUDE 83
SCOTT 84
BRIAN 85
SAMANTHA 87
ESTELLA 87
IN SUMMARY 89
FURTHER INFORMATION 90
ALCOHOLICS ANONYMOUS (A.A.) 90
NARCOTICS ANONYMOUS (NA) 94
ADDITIONAL SUPPORT GROUPS AND RESOURCES 94

CHAPTER 5 - THEME 5
TAKING RESPONSIBILITY 99
LARRY'S STORY 100
BOBBY'S STORY 104
RON'S STORY 109
CO-OCCURRING DISORDERS 111
YOUNG ADULTS AND CO-OCCURRING DISORDERS 112
RODRIGO'S FAMILY'S STORY 113
FURTHER INFORMATION 116
FAMILY AND MENTAL HEALTH RESOURCES 116

CHAPTER 6 - THEME 6
WILLINGNESS TO CHANGE: PREPARATION TO CHANGE ... 119
- *JANET'S STORY* ... 120
- STAGES OF CHANGE ... 122
- PREP FOR SUCCESS ... 124
  - *DANIEL'S STORY* ... 125
- PREPARATION FOR ABSTINENCE ... 127
- EXAMPLES OF WILLINGNESS ... 129
- FURTHER INFORMATION ... 130
  - *SMART RECOVERY* ... 130
- AN APOLOGY ... 132
- BOOK RECOMMENDATION ... 134

CHAPTER 7 - THEME 7
ACTION TO CHANGE ... 139
- *MARILYN'S STORY* ... 140
- THE ACTIONS OF RECOVERY ... 142
  - *PEGGY'S STORY* ... 143
  - *THEIR STORIES CONTINUE* ... 146
- THE IMPORTANCE OF H.A.L.T. ... 146
- ACTIONS TO MANAGE H.A.L.T. ... 147
- SECOND GEAR ... 149
- S.E.T. THE DAY ... 150
- LATER STAGE ACTIONS ... 152
- IN SUMMARY ... 153
- FURTHER INFORMATION ... 154

WOMEN FOR SOBRIETY, INC. 154

CHAPTER 8 - THEME 8
ACCOUNTABILITY AND THE GROWTH
OF EMPATHY 159
- ACCOUNTABILITY TOOLS 161
- AN EMPLOYEE 162
- ACCOUNTABILITY AND RELAPSE
  PREVENTION 163
  - *RAY'S STORY CONTINUES* 164
- EMPATHY 166
  - *ALONSO'S STORY* 167
  - *ALONSO UPDATE* 171
  - *THE DEER IN NARA* 171
- **FURTHER INFORMATION** 173
  - *SECULAR ORGANIZATIONS FOR*
    SOBRIETY (SOS) 173

PARADIGM 3   SELF-REGULATION 177

CHAPTER 9 - THEME 9
FORGIVENESS AND ACCEPTING
CONSEQUENCES 179
- FORGIVING SELF 182
- NELSON MANDELA MODELS
  FORGIVENESS 183
  - *THE POWER OF FORGIVENESS* 184
  - *USING FORGIVENESS TO HELP HIS*
    NATION HEAL 186
- CLIENTS AND FORGIVENESS 189

- RAY'S STORY CONTINUES 189
- ESTELLA'S STORY CONTINUES 191
- FURTHER INFORMATION 193
  - JOURNALING 193

CHAPTER 10 - THEME 10
SELF-REGULATION 197
- THE THREE RS 199
  - RITUALS 199
  - ROUTINES 200
  - RESOURCES 201
- THE GROWTH ZONE 202
- THE BALANCE WHEEL 202
- CO-OCCURRING DISORDERS 203
- FLEXIBLE THINKING, MANAGED EMOTIONS, MODERATE BEHAVIOR 204
- CHECKING YOURSELF 206
  - BRIAN'S STORY CONTINUES 207
- UTILIZING E.A.R. TECHNIQUES 212
- FURTHER INFORMATION 214
  - A BODY-CENTERED APPROACH TO RECOVERY 214
- TAPPING 216

CHAPTER 11 - THEME 11
MINDFULNESS 219
- CLASSIC MINDFULNESS MEDITATION TECHNIQUES 222

THE COLLECTIVE WISDOM OF RECOVERY

A DAY IN THE LIFE OF PETER 223
MISSED OPPORTUNITIES 225
PRACTICE GRATITUDE 228
    DEBORAH'S STORY CONTINUES 229
GRATITUDE - AFFIRMATION - JOURNALING 231
    FURTHER INFORMATION 232
        BOOK RECOMMENDATIONS 232

PARADIGM 4; THEME 4 TRANSFORMATION 235

CHAPTER 12 - PUTTING IT ALL TOGETHER 235
    A MOMENT WITH HALEY 237
    MEETING JESSICA 238
    COFFEE WITH CAROLE 241
    JOHN'S COMMITMENT AND VISION 242
FURTHER INFORMATION FOR CLIENTS IN INDIVIDUAL THERAPY 247
    PARADIGM 1: PROBLEM RECOGNITION 248
    PARADIGM 2: TAKING RESPONSIBILITY 248
    PARADIGM 3: SELF-REGULATION 249
    PARADIGM 4: TRANSFORMATION 249
ABOUT THE AUTHOR 251
    BOOKS BY L. GEORGI DISTEFANO, LCSW 253

PARADIGM CHANGE

ACKNOWLEDGEMENTS

First and foremost, I want to acknowledge my appreciation for the many clients I have worked with over the years who have shared their journeys and collective wisdom with me. It has been a privilege working with each of you. In the truest sense of the word, you are all the co-authors of this book.

I am indebted to my dear friend and former colleague, Nancy Massey. Nancy and I worked together managing the program at San Diego State University's Driving Under the Influence (DUI) Program for over 14 years. Nancy's assistance was instrumental in my first two textbooks on this topic. I decided to write a smaller book for the client interested in utilizing the Paradigm Developmental Model of Treatment (PDMT) with their therapist/counselor in individual therapy and was delighted when Nancy volunteered to assist me. This assistance has been invaluable. She has read every word of each draft, editing the manuscript and offering insight and encouragement throughout the process. Nancy has been incredibly dedicated to this project; I have been so touched by her generosity of time and effort.

I want to gratefully acknowledge my dear friend Marilynn Gould who was instrumental in helping me shape the narrative and complete my first draft. Marilynn's enthusiasm and unfailing support launched many months of work on this project.

A special thank you to another former colleague at SDSU and friend, Patricia Cabezas Churchill. Patricia was incredibly involved in bringing my first two textbooks on this topic to fruition. She is an IT wizard and was instrumental in all things technical for this project. In addition, Patricia translated my original textbook into Spanish. I doubt there's another person as knowledgeable about the PDMT Model. Patricia was relentless in pushing me to write this manuscript, for which I am truly grateful.

I want to thank and acknowledge Melanie Barker, MPH, LCSW, the current Executive/Clinical Director of the SDSU DUI Program. Melanie has worked tirelessly to teach the PDMT Model throughout the state of California to social workers, counselors, and therapists. She has been involved in the development of the model since the beginning and oversees the fidelity of this treatment approach at San Diego State University's Driving Under the Influence Program. Melanie's clinical direction and implementation of the model is highly regarded.

This book is the third collaboration with my editor Kim Mazyck at SDSU's Montezuma Publishing. Kim is a gem. Her sage advice and wisdom in shepherding this book have been immeasurable, and the staff at Montezuma has great energy and commitment. Their involvement in this publication is greatly appreciated. A special shout-out to Lia Dearborn. Her style and formatting contributed significantly to the clarity of the text. Her cover design is inspired and truly captures the essence of the topic. Many thanks.

My friend and frequent co-author Bill Eddy has been a source of continual encouragement. Bill is a prolific writer with over 10 books to his credit. Our friendship goes back over 30 years when we both worked as social workers at a hospital's chemical dependency program. Bill went on to become an attorney and an international speaker on high-conflict personalities. I appreciate his counsel and collaboration. In this book, I discuss several of the self-regulation techniques we wrote about in another publication.

Finally, I am indebted to Doris, my spouse and life partner of 42 years, who not only contended with my intense writing schedule but also graciously stepped in to assist me in managing multiple demands on a daily basis. Doris is also an experienced social worker who has spent over 35 years working in the field of addiction treatment at various chemical dependency programs both in New York and California. Her insight and wisdom in writing this book has been invaluable.

PARADIGM CHANGE

FOREWORD

After completing only three chapters of the book, my immediate view moved from it being ONLY about recovery from substance abuse, but a truly accurate confirmation of the author's statement: "The paradigm themes can be considered a design for living because as each theme unfolds, we understand more about ourselves and make healthy adjustments and choices based on our new set of priorities, intentions, and commitments."

This goal is, indeed, a noble one for those in addiction recovery. It goes far beyond and can be inclusive of helping those persons struggling with a host of life's challenging issues and problems. It introduced me to one of the most promising recovery approaches I have known in the 45 years I have devoted to the substance abuse field.

Reading the book is an educational experience. Case after case cited in detail will give hope to those persons needing help. These cases will also stimulate professionals to consider the use of the Paradigm Developmental Model of Treatment (PDMT), described in the book, as an addition to any treatment in use or as a total recovery paradigm change.

My hope is for this book to become widely used in treatment centers and educational institutions preparing students and professionals to work in the addiction field. I also advocate its use as a prescription for helping individuals move from active addiction and other related problems to living in recovery and reclaiming their potential for health and happiness.

Frances L. Brisbane Ph.D., MSW,
Vice President, Health Sciences Workforce Diversity
Office of Faculty, Staff and Student Diversity; and
Professor, School of Social Welfare
(Former Dean, School of Social Welfare)
Stony Brook University, Stony Brook, New York

A NOTE TO READERS

This book contains the opinion and ideas of its author. It is not intended to be a substitute for a professional diagnosis, medical treatment, or therapy. The reader should consult his or her physician or qualified mental health provider with any questions regarding medical or mental health symptoms or concerns. Detoxification may require medical management and the reader should not attempt a detoxification without physician consultation and supervision.

The author and publisher specifically disclaim responsibility for any liability, loss, or problem which is incurred as a consequence—directly or indirectly—regarding the use and application of any of the contents of this book.

INTRODUCTION

PARADIGM CHANGE

I have been a therapist for over forty years and have specialized in two areas of treatment, one of which is substance abuse/addiction treatment. I have met many remarkable people and I have been privileged to assist them in their journey of recovery. As I prepare for retirement, it occurred to me that I have the knowledge shared by my clients that could be of value to others. Over the years I have passed this wisdom from one client to the next. I have come to call this knowledge "Collective Wisdom," an assortment of insights, tips, and practical advice that many have found useful in their own journey of recovery. This book is my attempt to pass on this information to a larger circle of people who might benefit from this collective wisdom.

For nearly two decades I taught newly licensed social workers about chemical dependency treatment. Often, they were at a loss as to how to assist clients who had just stopped using, and/or were attending Alcoholics Anonymous (A.A.), SMART Recovery, or another support group. To be truthful, they sometimes overwhelmed their new clients by focusing prematurely on their childhood or other relationships rather than focusing on the here and now, step-by-step, cognitive/behavioral aspects of recovery.

To address this issue, in 2007 I developed a treatment approach called The Paradigm Developmental Model of Treatment (PDMT) and outlined the model in the publication *Alcoholism Treatment Quarterly* [1]. It provides a cognitive-behavioral and secular interpretation of the Twelve Steps of Alcoholics Anonymous [2]. Let me be clear, this model is not intended to replace the traditional Twelve Steps. I respect the A.A. program immensely and have firsthand knowledge of its many success stories.

INTRODUCTION

Nevertheless, the PDMT Model serves a useful treatment purpose providing a cognitive-behavioral framework for counselors/therapists to discuss the developmental tasks of recovery with their clients, without focusing on the spiritual aspects. I believe that perspective is better left to sponsors or spiritual advisors. Also, for those individuals who do not want to engage in A.A. and have selected SMART Recovery or another support group (or no support group), it provides an alternative perspective that is cognitive and developmental in design.

In 2010, I co-wrote the book *The Paradigm Developmental Model of Treatment: A Clinical Guide for Counselors Working with Substance Abusers and the Chemically Dependent* [3] with Melinda Hohman, Ph.D. Mindy is the current Director of the School of Social Work at San Diego State University. It was followed in 2012 by my book, *The Paradigm Developmental Model of Treatment Group Topics* [4]. Both of these large texts were written for counselors and therapists to use in their work with clients. They were designed to be used in both individual therapy and group treatment settings to help clients moderate their alcohol use or achieve sobriety and manage their first years of recovery.

In the excellent book *Sober for Good,* author Anne M. Fletcher cites research to make the point that there are many roads to recovery [5]. In addition to inpatient and outpatient treatment programs, some individuals utilize Moderation Management, SMART Recovery, Women for Sobriety, Inc., Secular Organization for Sobriety (SOS), individual counseling, faith-based programs, self-management, A.A., or any combination. The PDMT is designed to help individuals consider issues that will impact their ability to moderate their use or get clean and sober, regardless of which support group or method they utilize.

The premise of the PDMT is straightforward. As an individual grows in recovery and self-understanding, their thinking changes. We call these changes paradigm shifts. Collectively, the paradigm themes can be considered a design for living because as each theme unfolds, we understand more about ourselves and make healthy adjustments and choices based on our new set of priorities, intentions, and commitments.

The first paradigm is "Problem Recognition." "Do I, or do I not, have a problem with alcohol or other drugs (AOD)?" Within this first paradigm are three key themes, a secular variation of the first three steps of A.A.:

- Theme #1 - Problem Recognition (also the title of the Paradigm)
- Theme #2 - Looking Beyond Self
- Theme #3 - Letting Go

Exploring these first three themes as a person attempts to moderate their use or become clean and sober will establish the basis for this developmental journey [3]. It is critical for a person to recognize they have a problem before they become willing to do something about it. Individuals tend to minimize, excuse, or deny the impact of alcohol/drugs on their lives. Therefore, they often will remain resistant toward accepting they have any significant problem. Even when a person confirms they have an AOD problem, they still might not want to become abstinent. Working on these first three themes not only addresses the question, "to what extent do I have a problem?" but also the questions, "should I look beyond myself to help manage this problem?" and "what

INTRODUCTION

preconceived ideas about my AOD use do I need to 'let go'?"

Individuals attempting moderation management will continue to focus on these three themes as they evaluate their relationship with alcohol or other drugs. If a person can successfully moderate their use, they may wish to work in therapy on the remaining paradigm themes to strengthen their coping skills and ability to self-regulate in other areas of their lives.

For other individuals who have initiated abstinence, the next set of paradigm themes occur. The second paradigm is "Taking Responsibility." Now that a person has achieved abstinence, how do they manage it? Within this paradigm are five themes which I believe are essential to strengthen the resiliencies necessary for ongoing recovery:

- Theme #4 - Self-Examination
- Theme #5 – Taking Responsibility (also the title of the Paradigm)
- Theme #6 - Willingness/Preparation
- Theme #7 - Action to Change
- Theme #8 - Accountability/Empathy

A successful early recovery process can benefit greatly by addressing these themes. Why? These themes move a person from thinking about a problem (cognitive) to doing something about it (behavioral) [3]. As you often hear in the community, you cannot think your way out of this disease: you must take action. These themes are developmental in that you contemplate changes, prepare for changes, and finally make those changes [6].

Paradigm 3 represents a still deeper shift in thinking and is titled "Self-Regulation and Embracing

Change." The themes in this paradigm are essential for the continued self-management of your recovery. The themes in Paradigm 3 are:
- Theme #9 - Forgiveness and Accepting Consequences
- Theme #10 - Self-Regulation (also the title of the paradigm)
- Theme #11 - Mindfulness

Usually, it is at this point that an individual focuses on maintaining the gains made in sobriety by utilizing relapse prevention tools, growth goals, and other strategies to maintain a healthy balance and equilibrium in their daily life [3].

The fourth paradigm and final theme is "Transformation." Individuals who have addressed their personal issues, learned to self-regulate in consistently healthy ways, and become completely comfortable in their sobriety have achieved a personal transformation. They often are involved in passing on what they have learned and accomplished. Some remain very active in self-help groups or become sponsors, counselors, or volunteers. They recognize for their sobriety the importance and value of giving back [3].

For a number of years, I have worked with clients utilizing these themes in individual weekly therapy. This book contains the "Collective Wisdom" we have learned from their journeys.

I recommend discussing the themes outlined in this book with a counselor or therapist, as either can be a powerful ally as an individual addresses recovery. However, if that is not an option, I attempted to make this text as self-explanatory and clear as possible. This book

INTRODUCTION

is also useful for individuals with longer-term sobriety. A focus on Paradigms 2 and 3 can be a valuable experience and enhance quality recovery.

I have treated scores of clients over the years, and the stories included here are based on actual client histories. However, in order to protect and ensure complete confidentiality, identifying information has been changed and story content interchanged. In some cases, the client is a composite in order to illustrate a point. In all cases, the "Collective Wisdom" was something meaningful and life altering for the client.

On the final page of this Introduction is a graph that illustrates the twelve PDMT themes and the paradigm shifts I will discuss.

I have also added a FURTHER INFORMATION section to the end of each chapter to provide definitions, self-help resources, reading recommendations, medication information, and other data that may help to clarify the material or provide further information.

For those individuals who will be using the PDMT Model in individual counseling, I have included references to exercises and activities from my textbook, *The Paradigm Developmental Model of Treatment* [3]. If your therapist works with this model, they will have copies of these exercises/activities on a disc in the back of their book. The book also includes a clinical manual that is designed to use with clients. These materials should help to enrich your understanding of the themes as they apply to your life.

On a final note, let me say that much of what I have learned about addiction has come not only from successes but from engaging with individuals who lost their battle—either permanently or temporarily—with alcohol and other drugs. It is my hope that in relating their experiences, we can extract something worthwhile that would be of benefit to others.

I strongly believe that we must remain open to new research and treatment information. The field of addiction medicine is changing as we learn more about the brain and the role of chemical processes. The most important piece of "Collective Wisdom" I have learned as a therapist is that "NOT ONE SIZE FITS ALL." Treatment should be tailored to provide options to clients depending on a variety of factors. New and effective advances in medication provide new resources that once were not available. There are also a number of support groups in addition to A.A., such as SMART Recovery, that deserve to be respected and promoted in treatment settings. Further, many individuals can benefit from managing and reinforcing their recovery with therapy long after initial stabilization has occurred.

I hope this book will prove useful to whatever options you choose to consider.

INTRODUCTION

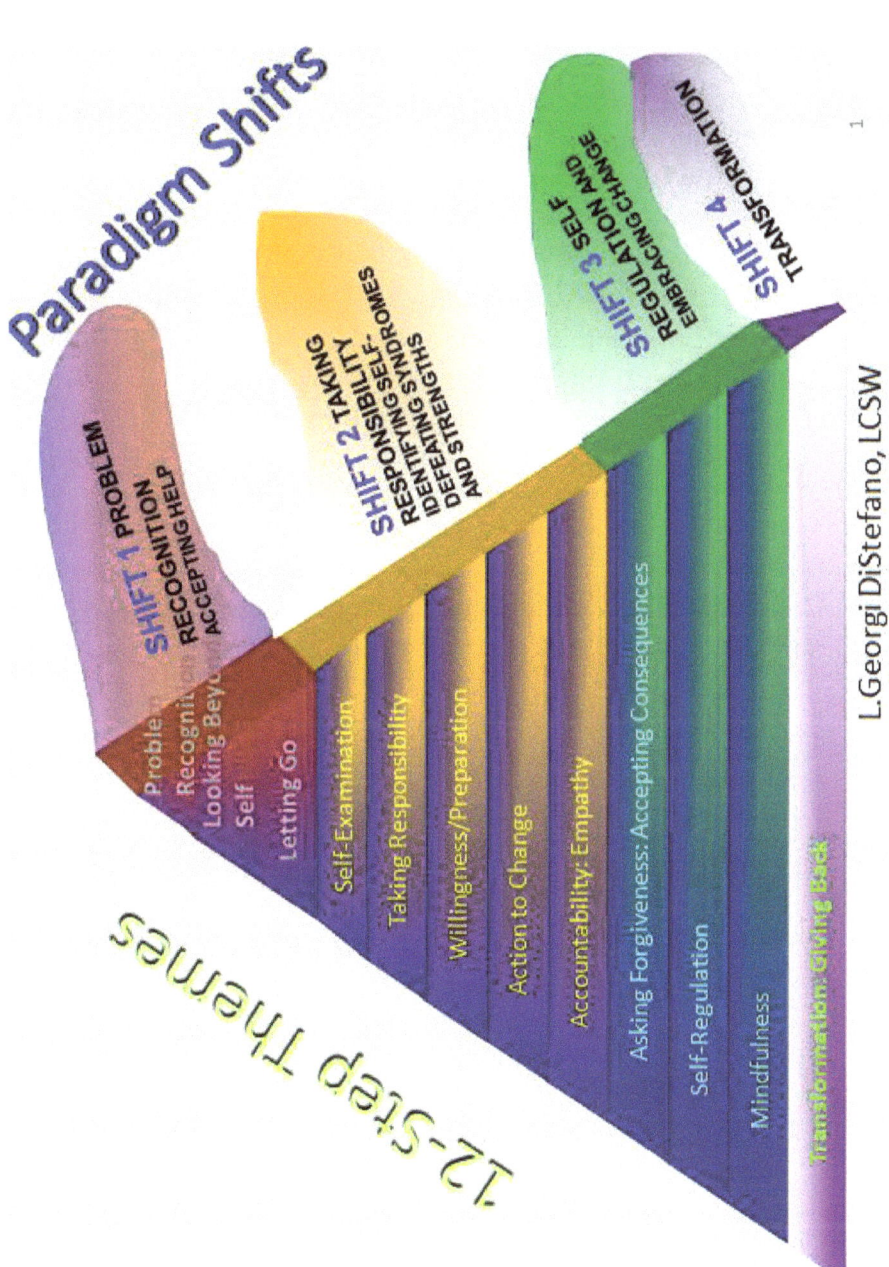

REFERENCE LIST

[1]   L.G. DiStefano, LCSW and M. Hohman, Ph.D., "Paradigm Developmental Model of Treatment: A Framework for Treating DUI Offenders," *Alcoholism Treatment Quarterly*, volume 25, no. 3, 2007.

[2]   Alcoholics Anonymous World Services, Inc. (2016 August). *The Twelve Steps of Alcoholics Anonymous* [Online]. Available: http://www.aa.org/assets/en_US/smf-121_en.pdf

[3]   L.G. DiStefano, LCSW and M. Hohman, Ph.D., *The Paradigm Developmental Model of Treatment: A Clinical Guide for Counselors Working with Substance Abusers and the Chemically Dependent.* San Diego, CA: Montezuma Publishing, 2010.

[4]   L.G. DiStefano, LCSW, *The Paradigm Developmental Model of Treatment Group Topics.* San Diego, CA: Montezuma Publishing, 2012.

[5]   A.M. Fletcher, *Sober for Good: New Solutions for Drinking Problems—Advice from Those Who Have Succeeded.* Boston, MA: Houghton Mifflin, 2001.

[6]   University of Rhode Island, Cancer Research Center. (2017). *Detailed Overview of the Transtheoretical Model of Change* [Online]. Available: http://web.uri.edu/cprc/detailed-overview/

PROLOGUE

TRANSFORMATION

I remember a crisp fall day in San Diego in the mid '90s as I made my way to a beautiful old church in a nearby community. It was hard to believe all the people who were there. The crowd spilled out of the church; it was an amazing sight. I had the privilege of giving the eulogy that day and my mind drifted back to over a decade before when I first met Ray.

RAY'S STORY

I was a social worker on an inpatient chemical dependency unit of a local hospital. Although Ray was new to the program, he had had two previous hospitalizations for alcoholism at other facilities. At 66 years old he was hard headed, set in his ways, and often less than pleasant. His devoted wife Lynn dreaded her upcoming retirement. Life was a series of painful routines. She would come home to find Ray already drunk and nasty. She would make him dinner, which was often accompanied by a tirade, only to put him to bed several hours later and begin the whole soul-numbing routine again the following day.

Ray completed the three-week program at the insistence of his wife and her brother. However, the odds of his success appeared poor. He had little motivation, insight, or true desire to change his life.

In those days, the hospital doctors would give referrals to the social work staff for their private practice, generally for one of two reasons: either the patient was exceptionally difficult or lacked the money/insurance for ongoing treatment. While Ray was fortunate enough to have the resources after having retired from a long career with the post office, he fell in the category of "exceptionally difficult".

PROLOGUE - TRANSFORMATION

So, soon after his hospital discharge, he began to see me for therapy. I instinctively recognized that Ray would have difficulty with the intimacy involved in individual therapy. Additionally, it was clear that the more tools and support his wife had in coping with his chronic disease, the more likely a successful outcome. I should note that his wife was an active weekly Al-Anon member and had been for many years. The three of us began to meet for what we called family therapy.

I knew that Ray had a horrible childhood. His mother had been a prostitute, and he often could not come home at night until her business was complete. She treated him very poorly, exposing him to seedy characters and drugs.

He never knew his father, whom his mother often referred to with disdain and anger. Ray endured many lonely days, especially holidays (remember this). He managed to graduate high school, and—like many men of his generation—joined the service. He loved the opportunity and structure the service offered, and he thrived. Unfortunately, Ray was introduced to alcohol and began drinking with his buddies. He thoroughly enjoyed the camaraderie and sense of family he felt. After his honorable discharge, he applied and found employment at the post office. Again, he liked the structure and routine.

He met and married Lynn, and they had one son together. According to Lynn, Ray and their son Jack were close during the child's elementary school years, but as Ray's drinking increased they became increasingly estranged. The son eventually moved across the country to be as far away as possible from the "craziness" at home.

The initial deal I made with Ray was that he must take the medication Antabuse (disulfiram) daily, in front of his wife, for us to work together. Antabuse was the first medication approved for alcohol abuse [1]. Given that his past attempts post-hospitalization were failures, he reluctantly agreed to the treatment contract. He understood that Antabuse never stopped anyone who wanted to return to drinking. A person needs to wait several days till the medication is out of their system to drink again. The value of Antabuse is that it is a tool and can be effective in managing short term urges and impulses (remember this).

Another requirement was a minimum of three A.A. meetings per week. Fortunately, Ray did not have strong feelings against the program; he just did not attend on a consistent basis nor did he work steps (A.A. Twelve Steps) or have an A.A. sponsor. We addressed those issues over time.

Surprisingly, weeks turned into months, and Ray remained sober. I realized one day before his session that I was actually looking forward to seeing him. His wife could not believe the changes she was witnessing. Now when she returned home from work, he had a meal ready for her! Ray had become a very proficient cook. Additionally, the house was picked up, and he would discuss the news of the day at dinner. He faithfully attended meetings and had selected an experienced sponsor. They began working the steps.

One day to my surprise Ray showed up at the hospital alumni meeting. He volunteered to open his home for patients who had nowhere to go for the holidays. In those days, insurance allowed us to give patients passes from the hospital for a daytime event or

PROLOGUE - TRANSFORMATION

activity. True to his word, Ray and Lynn hosted countless alcohol/drug-free holiday parties for hospital patients and alumni in recovery who wanted a safe, warm, and loving home in which to celebrate. For many years we (the hospital program) attempted to reimburse Ray for his considerable expenses. Whenever the subject came up, he would grin and say "Are you kidding? Do you realize how much money I am saving by not drinking?"

Ray became a fixture at several weekly A.A. meetings. So much so that when he became seriously ill, the location of the meeting was moved to Ray's home so that he could attend. Here was a guy who did not have a friend in the world when we first met, who within a decade became a beloved member of both the A.A. and hospital Alumni communities. As a matter of fact, once when he and his wife Lynn returned from an anniversary vacation to Hawaii, so many people showed up at the airport to welcome them home that the airport security thought a celebrity had arrived.

I was a young therapist when I began working with Ray. In those days, I had a wonderful clinical supervisor (psychiatrist) to guide my therapeutic work. He agreed that Ray's recovery was nothing short of remarkable. He not only remained clean and sober but continued to grow as a man, husband, and father. The transformation we all witnessed with Ray was real and long lasting.

Perhaps the greatest gift working with Ray gave me was a profound respect for the fellowship of A.A. and the Twelve Steps. As a therapist, I have come to strongly support individuals working with whichever support program or method they choose. This does not, however, diminish my appreciation for the extraordinary recoveries I have seen occur with the A.A. program. I will discuss more about Ray in upcoming chapters.

START WITH THE END IN MIND

"Transformation" is the final paradigm and theme of the PDMT Model [2]. It occurs when an individual has a true integration of the 12 cognitive-behavioral themes. At this stage, a person experiences profound balance and equilibrium in their life. This is not to say that problems don't occur. Life has problems and challenges and can throw us curve balls. But now the individual has the skill, insight, and emotional stability to handle whatever challenges they are confronted with constructively.

Back in 1978, author Chaney Allen wrote the famous book I'm Black and I'm Sober [3]. Chaney, a minister's daughter, tells her story about fighting the disease of alcoholism. She pointed out in an interview regarding that book that "sobriety is not the answer to all life's problems [4:p.22]." She wrote more extensively on this topic in the book *Life Goes on Drunk or Sober* [5]. Frustrating, difficult, unpleasant, and sad things still happen. The difference is that with sobriety, a person is much more capable of effective problem-solving."

When an individual has reached the stage of transformation, they truly think and behave differently. They have become a different person emotionally because they have learned to manage life in a way that protects their sobriety and supports their resiliencies, regardless of the challenges that life throws at them. Transformation represents a significant change in the way an individual sees him or herself and the world. There are many paths to recovery and a transformative process. I hope the following pages will help to explain one way to reach transformation for those who are on this journey.

REFERENCE LIST

[1] NIH: National Institute on Alcohol Abuse and Alcoholism. (2016, March). *Medications Development Program: Disulfiram (Antabuse®)* [Online]. Available: https://www.niaaa.nih.gov/research/major-initiatives/medications-development-program

[2] L.G. DiStefano, LCSW and M. Hohman, Ph.D, *The Paradigm Developmental Model of Treatment: A Clinical Guide for Counselors Working with Substance Abusers and the Chemically Dependent.* San Diego, CA: Montezuma Publishing, 2010.

[3] C. Allen, *I'm Black and I'm Sober: A Minister's Daughter Tells Her Story about Fighting the Disease of Alcoholism and Winning.* Minneapolis, MN: Compcare Publications, 1978.

[4] "Chaney: I'm Black and I'm Sober," The Star-News, p. 22 [Chula Vista] May 9, 1985.

[5] C. Allen, *Life goes on Drunk or Sober!* San Diego, CA: Chaney Allen Enterprises, 1986.

PARADIGM CHANGE

PARADIGM 1
PROBLEM RECOGNITION

PARADIGM CHANGE

CHAPTER 1

THEME 1
PROBLEM RECOGNITION

PARADIGM 1: PROBLEM RECOGNITION

The first paradigm consists of three themes: Problem Recognition, Looking Beyond Self, and Letting Go. In this paradigm, individuals are examining their relationship with alcohol and/or other drugs to determine the extent of their problem. Problem recognition and the acceptance of appropriate help are the key themes of this paradigm [1].

THEME 1: PROBLEM RECOGNITION

"ARE YOU A PICKLE OR ARE YOU A CUCUMBER?"

In the late 1980s, I opened an outpatient chemical dependency treatment program with the well-regarded psychiatrist, Raymond Fidaleo M.D. Our facility was located in a beautiful, old, historic home located in the Bankers Hill area of San Diego. We had both day and evening treatment programs. Group therapy was a major and powerful component of treatment. To be honest, I cannot recall how the routine began, but whenever a new person was considering joining the program, we invited them to meet the group. During this initial visit, a veteran of the group would place an actual jar of pickles on the coffee table in the center of the room. He/she would then tell the newcomer the story of the pickle and the cucumber:

"You see, if you take a cucumber and put it into a mixture of brine, at some point it turns into a pickle. Try as hard as it might, it can never be a cucumber again. If you are addicted, you're like the pickle: you are trying very hard to be a cucumber. But, if you're addicted to

1 - PROBLEM RECOGNITION

alcohol or other drugs, it probably won't work. So, this is a program for pickles. It's important to recognize whether you have a problem or not, because it takes a lot of work and effort to be clean and sober. You would be crazy to want to do all that work if you didn't have a real problem. So if you decide to join, you will need to explain to the group why you think you have a serious problem. We don't care what your spouse, or your doctor, or your family think. We care what you think!"

Problem Recognition is the first of the clinical themes I have outlined in the PDMT. It corresponds to, but is different than, the first step of A.A.: "We admitted we were powerless over alcohol—that our lives had become unmanageable [2]."

Over the years I have treated hundreds of individuals with substance abuse issues. Since the days of talking about pickles and cucumbers in treatment programs, we have come to recognize that alcohol and substance abuse issues run on a spectrum from mild to severe.

Some individuals cut down on consumption, moderate their use, and appear to have stabilized their lives. Others engage in harm-reduction activities like not drinking daily or not drinking and driving in an attempt to reduce their chances of serious consequences.

However, others have recognized a significant problem that will require abstinence. This group recognizes they are powerless over alcohol, though some individuals are not comfortable with that conceptualization. Problem recognition as a PDMT theme is inclusive of this spectrum.

In regard to deciding to be abstinent, author Anne M. Fletcher, in her excellent book *Sober for Good*, states,

"I believe this commitment to abstinence represents a paradigm shift in thinking [3:p.81]." She further states, "The paradigm shift for these masters occurred when they stopped seeing themselves as people who might eventually be able to control their use of alcohol, if only they tried a little harder, and began to see themselves as people who no longer drank. They started to regard themselves as nondrinkers, making an inner (and sometimes outward) commitment never to drink again and to change their lives accordingly [3:p.81]."

According to the literature, 40 percent of individuals who know they have an alcohol or drug problem are not ready to stop using [4]. However, they may be willing to talk about the issue and consider medication resources and/or a moderation approach. Working with an individual counselor in a safe and supportive environment can be extremely useful before a person is ready to make any change to their behavior or lifestyle.

According to Ms. Fletcher's research, "Having counseling with someone other than a chemical dependency (CD) counselor was one of the top three ways in which the masters resolved their drinking problems. (Having CD counseling wasn't far behind [3:p.81].)"

If an individual decides they want to be clean and sober, an inpatient or outpatient treatment program can be an invaluable support. Going directly to a 12-step fellowship or other self-help group is also an option for those who may not have the resources or desire for a formal treatment option.

Clients often describe their treatment programs like boot camp. In a short period of time, an individual is taught many skills to help successfully manage addiction.

1 - PROBLEM RECOGNITION

A person can certainly learn these tools and skills in self-help environments, but program treatment will hopefully ensure exposure, in a systematic way, to the components of recovery management. Self-help programs can then reinforce or add to one's body of knowledge and support the behavioral changes that person wants to make. Individual counseling following program treatment can be extremely helpful in implementing and monitoring the changes necessary to sustain sobriety. Following are some stories to illustrate these points.

SCOTT'S STORY

A therapist who was relocating to the East Coast referred Scott to me. He had been in therapy with her for about one year and had completed a well-regarded outpatient treatment program. Scott was 47 when he began to work with me. He was a successful entrepreneur with a small business. He was recently divorced with a college-age daughter. His self-described goal for continued counseling was that he wanted his fifties to be successful, productive, and healthy. Although Scott appeared to genuinely like SMART Recovery, his attendance was sporadic. Scott was extremely gregarious and enjoyed an active physical lifestyle that unfortunately involved a golf club and friends who drank regularly. At first, he attempted to abstain, however within four months he was back to drinking. He then made efforts to manage consumption and reduce negative consequences but refused to consider medication like naltrexone as a resource. A series of relationships followed and the most serious was with a woman with a significant alcohol problem. In comparison, Scott saw his consumption as moderate until it was pointed out that the goal posts had changed. Compared to his girlfriend his drinking was less, but it was not inconsequential. Scott struggled with this dilemma over the course of three years while making significant gains in other areas and finally broke off the relationship with his alcoholic girlfriend. He eventually met a woman who appeared much healthier and who drank far less. Nevertheless, Scott would drink moderately for weeks and sometimes months, but would on occasion binge drink, get drunk, and create very unpleasant consequences for himself. On one occasion, he locked himself out of his home. On another occasion, a fight they had over her ex-boyfriend (while drinking) resulted in Scott storming off in his car, only to be arrested for his second DUI in under 10 years. The consequences were significant. There were no physical injuries or property damages, nevertheless the huge financial impact on both his resources and his ability to work were enormous.

Scott was philosophical after the arrest, "I have only myself to blame. I knew I was playing with fire!" Fortunately, the arrest helped to refocus Scott on engaging in recovery. The DUI requirements and license restrictions were a constant reminder of his situation. Scott said something else that I have heard from countless others. I believe it is part of the "Collective Wisdom" that is valuable to be passed on. He said, "WHENEVER I TRY TO NEGOTIATE WITH THIS DISEASE, I LOSE."

This is a powerful statement. As I stated earlier in this chapter, some people can cut back on consumption or engage in activities of harm reduction in a successful way. However, if you feel you have crossed the line and have a moderate to severe substance use disorder "Collective Wisdom" tells us that "HALF MEASURES

1 - PROBLEM RECOGNITION

WON'T WORK." *Scott learned you cannot successfully negotiate with this disease for any significant period of time.*

IT TAKES WHAT IT TAKES

Problem recognition is not always easy despite what may appear obvious. The following story demonstrates this point.

CLAUDE'S STORY

Claude came into treatment at the age of 78. Several months before, he broke his neck from a serious fall while intoxicated. He endured a nine-hour operation and was fortunate not to be paralyzed. Claude was married to Sally, his third wife, for over 30 years. Together they have two adult sons. In our first session, Claude acknowledged his alcoholism and desire to maintain his marriage and health in retirement. He did not want to attend a group treatment program but agreed to weekly individual sessions for one year, regular self-help meetings, and taking the medication Antabuse. This medication will get you seriously ill if you should drink; it is a recovery tool that requires a medical prescription and monitoring by a physician.

I frequently do what I call a "Consequence History" with clients. They complete a form that reviews their drinking/drug history over the course of their life. Since Claude was elderly, I suspected his history was going to be very interesting. It certainly was. We reviewed his drinking patterns over several decades and the numerous consequences he experienced.

At 16, Claude was drinking with a cousin and some friends. He raced his car down a windy mountain, lost control, rolled, and totaled the car. Everyone survived the accident with varying degrees of injury. At the age of 19, while in the military, he became intoxicated and got involved in a serious fight with buddies from his Marine platoon against another group of soldiers. He barely avoided a dishonorable discharge.

In his late 20s, after drinking and driving, he became sleepy on the San Francisco Bay Bridge hitting the curb with his wheel and barely avoided a major crash. Additional stories filled out Claude's history. He drove drunk with his two young children in the car, frightening them terribly. On a Canadian vacation, he fell asleep drunk in a hot tub and almost drowned. Fortunately, his wife found and revived him. On another occasion, he smashed his face into a computer after an evening of drinking. Claude acknowledged that his drinking resulted in many poor decisions, including two failed marriages.

I list all these consequences—and there were more—to demonstrate that many people would have experienced a wake-up call with any one of those events. Nearly driving off a bridge or endangering the lives of your children might have been enough to motivate someone else into treatment. Often these types of situations do just that. Denial and minimization break and a person obtains a clarity about their plight. However, it takes what it takes, and for Claude it took a broken neck at the age of 78 and a wife who said, "Enough, get treatment or move out" to get him to finally take action.

Today Claude has been clean and sober for over two years. I asked him recently what "Collective Wisdom" was most valuable to him. He replied, "LEARNING AND REPEATING THE MANTRA THAT DRINKING IS NO LONGER AN OPTION." While he works consistently on his recovery and attends self-help (SMART Recovery) very frequently, Claude stated that it was this change in his thinking process that has helped him the most.

DEBORAH'S STORY

I worked with Deborah for several years after she completed both inpatient and outpatient treatment programs for opioid addiction, known medically as Opioid Use Disorder. She was addicted to Percocet and Vicodin. (The opioid in Percocet is oxycodone, and the opioid in Vicodin is hydrocodone [5].) Deborah was a physician enrolled in a diversion program and was motivated to save her medical license. She was a highly regarded surgeon and her dependency was not discovered by the hospital where she regularly worked, or because a patient or colleague initiated a complaint. An observant pharmacist reported her, after realizing Deborah was writing prescriptions in the names of others and picking them up for herself.

It was incredulous how many Percocet or Vicodin Deborah would take in the course of a day and still perform surgery. She had developed an incredible "tolerance" to the opioids.

Tolerance is "a decrease in response to a drug dose that occurs with continued use. Increased doses of the drug are required to achieve the effects originally produced by lower doses [6:p.644]". While most people would be feeling considerably impaired with more than the normal dose of 500 mg (one to two tablets every four to six hours), Deborah would take a handful of pills and appear normal to those around her.

Deborah met very strict treatment requirements and monitoring over a long period. She believes that *this accountability was an important ingredient in her success. Another factor that we will discuss in a subsequent chapter was Deborah's decision to leave her surgical practice, despite the fact that the medical board cleared her license.*

She had an enormous struggle at the beginning of her treatment. She detoxed at the hospital and was given naltrexone to suppress cravings. Today professionals utilize additional medications for this process.

Deborah understood that her brain chemistry was going to be compromised for a long time. With the staunch support of her husband and friends she created a strong support system in the Narcotics Anonymous/ Alcoholics Anonymous and physician community.

One day in a therapy session, Deborah expressed fear about the public learning of her addiction. I shook my head and said to her, "what I have learned from other recovering addicts is that YOU CAN'T SAVE YOUR ASS AND YOUR FACE AT THE SAME TIME."

She frequently told me how impactful that "Collective Wisdom" was to her. It helped to put her true priorities in perspective. Years have passed since that conversation, and today Deborah often speaks in public about her addiction and recovery.

Regarding problem recognition, Deborah was candid that she was completely aware that her opioid dependence was severe and detection would seriously jeopardize her career and marriage. Nevertheless, despite her vows to herself, she continued risky behavior, which increased over time. She based every decision on when she could use and how she could cover it up. She took greater and greater risks until the pharmacist caught her. Deborah stated that although she was terrified when they apprehended her, she was also immensely relieved because she realized she could not stop on her own.

A WORD ABOUT TRAUMA

Many people live in an emotional prison created during their childhoods. Alcoholism, drug addiction, trauma, neglect, violence, and other destructive forces create a "war zone" that children attempt to survive by adapting to the circumstances with which they are confronted. It is important to recognize that this adaptation was essential to their survival and helped them develop resilience.

These children enter adulthood still holding onto the defenses and responses that helped them survive. Now those responses and ways of interpreting the world can be counterproductive and limiting. Many of these individuals turn to alcohol and other drugs to cope and handle the stresses of everyday life. Many could benefit from a counseling process that finds the keys necessary to unlock the emotional confinement that restricts them.

The final paradigm of "Transformation" represents the psychological state of peace and equilibrium that truly occurs when an individual has been successful and is now free of the emotional restraints of the past. Watching clients work through the PDMT themes and embrace the changes that usher in a new lifestyle and relationship with their world is a joy and privilege. They are not perfect human beings; none of us are. But they work diligently to self-regulate, and that process produces a set of new, viable, and appropriate responses to the world.

Some individuals have to work through a specific trauma. I would highly recommend a competent cognitive-behavioral therapist to assist in that self-exploration.

Other individuals cannot pinpoint a specific traumatic event but have lived in a family "war zone" for so many years that they may have developed many of the signs, symptoms, and emotional responses associated with post-traumatic stress disorder (PTSD). They too need evaluation and assistance.

Many soldiers who develop PTSD from war experiences and do not have treatment for it, go on to develop problems with substance abuse. More than half of individuals who seek substance abuse treatment report one or more lifetime traumas. Additionally, a significant number of clients in inpatient treatment settings have traumatic stress symptoms or PTSD [7:p.9]. Addressing these issues in a safe therapeutic environment will go a long way in reinforcing recovery, supporting resilience, and freeing the individual to utilize a greater variety of healthy coping mechanisms.

A word of caution: before you engage in a deep exploration of childhood issues or trauma, select a therapist that you have checked out. Recommendations from insightful friends, work colleagues, or the employee assistance person at your employment can be invaluable.

Understand the therapist's credentials. You want a licensed cognitive-behavioral therapist who primarily treats individuals with substance use disorders. Many counselors have treated a few alcoholics or addicts over the course of their professional careers, but you want a therapist who predominantly specializes in this area and also utilizes the principles and approaches of Trauma-Informed Care (TCI). Why? Would you want to undergo surgery with someone who has done only a handful of heart or spinal surgeries over the course of their career or someone who performs several of these surgeries

1 - PROBLEM RECOGNITION

each and every week? There is no guarantee that the surgery will be better from the more experienced doctor, but the odds are it will. The more experienced person will probably have greater familiarity with the many nuances of the recovery process, be less likely to follow a cookie-cutter or dogmatic approach, and understand the implications of any trauma you have experienced.

Also, many individuals with addictions and those that have come from dysfunctional families often have a tendency not to take care of themselves or put their needs at the forefront. The very act of seeking assistance and vetting various professional options is a step in a new direction.

IN SUMMARY

While it's true that many individuals are not successful in initiating or maintaining successful sobriety, there are many who are. I have been privileged to work with a large number of individuals who have created wonderful lives in recovery. There is every reason to be hopeful. After you have recognized a problem with alcohol/drugs and secured treatment assistance, ask yourself the question, "what motivates me to want to be clean and sober?" or "what motivates me to want to cut down and moderate my alcohol/drug consumption?"

Some people will tell you that you have to do it completely for yourself. I take exception with that view. Over the years I've learned that different things motivate different people. So if you want to get clean to save a marriage, keep a job, or be a better parent, go ahead. If you want to quit because you are sick and tired of being sick and tired, go ahead and quit!

Interestingly, several years ago I asked a large group of recovering substance abuse counselors in a seminar with San Diego State University's DUI Program for the reasons they finally decided to stop. We wrote their responses on the whiteboard. Then I asked them why they have "remained" clean and sober. We wrote those responses on a different board. The reasons given for deciding to quit revolved around losses. People mentioned losses of marriages, health, homes, jobs, relationships, respect, etc. At some point, people cognitively and emotionally accepted that they could no longer pay the price or tolerate the losses of their addiction. When the group responded to the question why do they "remain" clean and sober, the reasons revolved around keeping what they valued. They spoke of loving their new lives, enjoying their children and marriages, valuing their work and colleagues, etc.

About a year after I did this exercise with these SDSU counselors, I was teaching the PDMT Model in Japan. One day I visited a recovery home in Osaka and asked a large group of their residents (with long-term recovery) the same two questions. Fascinatingly, the responses were almost identical. People appear to quit when the pain of the losses becomes untenable, but they remain clean and sober because they have a new appreciation for the gifts their recovery has given them. There is a reason you hear the term "grateful alcoholic or addict" in the community. The gratitude is real. Sustained recovery is not drudgery. The hope, optimism, and joy really do occur.

1 - PROBLEM RECOGNITION

FURTHER INFORMATION

Before any problem can be successfully resolved it first must be clearly recognized. This is especially true in responding effectively to substance misuse. Alcohol and drug misuse affects millions of people around the world. According to the United States Surgeon General in 2015, over 27 million people in the United States reported current use of illicit drugs or misuse of prescription drugs [4].

Recently, the American Psychiatric Association has changed the words we have historically used to describe problems with alcohol and other drugs. When someone becomes "hooked" on alcohol/drugs, we have used the word addiction, which I will continue to use as it is the most familiar term to the general public. However, the newest terminology is "substance use disorders" or "alcohol use disorder." The word addiction is no longer applied as a diagnostic term in the current Diagnostic and Statistical Manual (DSM-5) of the American Psychiatric Association [8:p.230]. Many professionals, including myself, question the wisdom and motivation behind this change. Nevertheless, the signs, symptoms, and progressive nature of the disease remain the same.

ALCOHOL USE DISORDER - DSM 5 DEFINITION [8:pp.233-234]

A problematic pattern of alcohol use leading to clinically significant impairment or distress as manifested by at least two of the following, occurring within a 12-month period:

1. Alcohol is often taken in larger amounts or over a longer period than was intended.

2. There is a persistent desire or unsuccessful efforts to cut down or control alcohol use.
3. A great deal of time is spent in activities necessary to obtain alcohol, use alcohol, or recover from its effects.
4. Craving, or a strong desire or urge to use alcohol.
5. Recurrent alcohol use resulting in a failure to fulfill major role obligations at work, school, or home.
6. Continued alcohol use despite having persistent or recurrent social or interpersonal problems caused or exacerbated by the effects of alcohol.
7. Important social, occupational, or recreational activities are given up or reduced because of alcohol use.
8. Recurrent alcohol use in situations in which it is physically hazardous.
9. Alcohol use is continued despite knowledge of having a persistent or recurrent physical or psychological problem that is likely to have been caused or exacerbated by alcohol.
10. Tolerance, as defined by either of the following:
    a. A need for markedly increased amounts of alcohol to achieve intoxication or desired effect.
    b. A markedly diminished effect with continued use of the same amount of alcohol.
11. Withdrawal, as manifested by either of the following:

1 - PROBLEM RECOGNITION

    a. The characteristic withdrawal syndrome for alcohol (see criteria for alcohol withdrawal).

    b. Alcohol (or a closely related substance, such as a Benzodiazepine) is taken to relieve or avoid withdrawal symptoms.

Please note that the DSM-5 uses the following severity scale:

    MILD: presence of 2-3 symptoms
    MODERATE: presence of 4-5 symptoms
    SEVERE: presence of 6 or more symptoms

REFERENCE LIST

[1]   L.G. DiStefano, LCSW and M. Hohman, Ph.D., *The Paradigm Developmental Model of Treatment: A Clinical Guide for Counselors Working with Substance Abusers and the Chemically Dependent.* San Diego, CA: Montezuma Publishing, 2010.

[2]   Alcoholics Anonymous World Services, Inc. (2016, Aug.). *The Twelve Steps of Alcoholics Anonymous* [Online]. Available: http://www.aa.org/assets/en_US/smf-121_en.pdf

[3]   A.M. Fletcher, *Sober for Good: New Solutions for Drinking Problems—Advice from Those Who Have Succeeded.* Boston, MA: Houghton Mifflin, 2001, p. 81.

[4]   Surgeon General. (2017). *Facing Addiction in America: The Surgeon General's Report on Alcohol, Drugs, and Health: Executive Summary* [Online]. Available: https://addiction.surgeongeneral.gov/executive-summary

[5]   NIH: National Institute on Drug Abuse. (2016, Jan). *Commonly Abused Drugs Charts: Prescription*

        Opioids [Online]. Available: https://www.drugabuse.gov/drugs-abuse/commonly-abused-drugs-charts#prescription-opioids

[6]   T. Nordegren, "Tolerance," in *The A-Z Encyclopedia of Alcohol and Drug Abuse*. Parkland, FL: Brown Walker Press, 2002, p. 644.

[7]   *Trauma-Informed Care in Behavioral Health Services: Quick Guide for Clinicians Based on TIP 57*, U.S. Department of Health and Human Services, Substance Abuse and Mental Health Services Administration, Rockville, MD, 2015, p. 9.

[8]   American Psychiatric Association, *Diagnostic and Statistical Manual of Mental Disorders,* 5th ed. Arlington, VA: American Psychiatric Association Publishing, 2013, pp. 230, 233-234.

CHAPTER 2

THEME 2
LOOKING BEYOND SELF

The second clinical theme of the PDMT model is Looking Beyond Self [1]. It's a cognitive interpretation of A.A.'s second step: "Came to believe that a Power greater than ourselves could restore us to sanity [2]." A spiritual belief in a higher power is the A.A. conception of this step. However, from a cognitive perspective, looking beyond your own thinking and personal resources can provide powerful tools as you grapple with substance abuse or addiction.

Many individuals get caught up in the God concept. Others, however, recognize that "a power greater than ourselves" can be the collective resources, knowledge, and support of the recovery community. You don't have to believe in God to benefit from the power of "Collective Wisdom," which is available at meetings, in recovery literature, online, and in counseling and treatment services.

We use the concept of Looking Beyond Self in much of our important decision making. If we want to improve our retirement investments, we may seek the assistance of a financial advisor. If we want to buy a new home, we may contact a real estate agent and ask them to guide us through the process. If we want to set up a will or trust, we go to a legal specialist. If we have a medical problem, seeing a doctor is the most common advice someone would give. So it follows that, if you have become aware of a problem or are concerned about your use of alcohol/drugs, it makes sense to expand your resources and knowledge to address whatever issue concerns you.

INSANITY

A frequently repeated saying in the recovery community is "doing the same thing over and over

2 - LOOKING BEYOND SELF

again and expecting a different result is the definition of insanity." Many people get stuck in a loop created by their own distorted thinking about their problem. As dependency on mood-altering chemicals increases, so does difficulty with judgment and clarity, so reaching out and engaging with others in recovery can be an essential lifeline. Brian's story demonstrates these points.

BRIAN'S STORY

In the spring of 2013, Brian was referred to my practice. He was 33 years old and the eldest child of the family. He has a younger brother and described his family with fond memories. His parents have had a good marriage. Unfortunately, Brian experienced a good deal of bullying in middle school and thus became quiet and withdrawn. His family was a source of support, nevertheless signs of depression began to emerge at age 13.

His beloved grandmother died at 14 and he became rebellious and, according to him, mean-spirited. He would frequently fly into a rage and engaged in various acts of vandalism and other acting out. At age 17 he discovered crystal meth, alcohol, and pot. After leaving home and moving out of state at the age of 22, his consumption increased markedly. In hindsight, he realized that he used crystal instead of addressing his depression and used alcohol and pot to level himself off.

Brian's family history is fraught with alcoholism. His paternal grandmother and uncle were alcoholic. His mother struggled with depression, and both of her parents had significant problems with alcohol although neither identified as alcoholic.

PARADIGM CHANGE

By age 30, Brian had lost a series of menial jobs, his driver's license was revoked, and he had spent numerous nights in jail. According to Brian, he promised himself on many occasions that he would stop. However, he failed in each of his attempts.

One day, when he realized there was nowhere else to turn, he went to an A.A. meeting, which led to entering a treatment program with the help of his parents. Upon discharge from the treatment program, Brian was advised not to return to his studio apartment. Fortunately, the clarity he had gained in treatment helped him make a very wise decision and he moved his possessions out of the apartment and went to live in a sober living recovery home for addicts and alcoholics. He lived in that sober living home for a full two years.

Frankly, Brian got lucky. He had a cat that he was devoted to. There are many sober living homes in California but very few that provide two to three-person apartments and allow clients to bring their personal pets. By removing the obstacle of leaving his pet, Brian was able to see the wisdom in the advice to enter a sober living situation.

While in sober living he continued on his antidepressant medication. Again, he was very lucky. In previous years, recovery homes and sober living facilities would not allow clients to be on antidepressant medication. Fortunately, they had grown with the times, acknowledged medical research, and had removed that restriction which created a major difficulty for many people in previous years.

Brian was lucky in a third respect: his exposure to counseling and his engagement in the A.A. program stirred in him a desire to be a drug and alcohol counselor,

2 - LOOKING BEYOND SELF

so he enrolled in a program at the local college. He also decided to continue in treatment to strengthen his relapse prevention plans and to gain greater insight into himself. That led to his initiation of therapy with me.

BREAKING THE VICIOUS CYCLE

When Brian reached his personal bottom (which is different for different people, like Claude and the multiple near disasters), he reached out and broke the vicious cycle of his own self-defeating behavior. He went to A.A., which led to a formal treatment program. That led to a psychiatrist and antidepressant medication. Those actions brought clarity and the all-important decision to live with others in a sober living environment. From these experiences, he decided to go to college and study to be an alcohol and drug counselor. That experience facilitated his thinking about counseling which led to weekly therapy during his recovery.

I will share more of Brian's story in subsequent chapters. It should be noted that Brian embraces the A.A. Twelve Steps and he strongly believes in a higher power. However, he felt the cognitive themes of the PDMT model were a positive and helpful adjunct as we worked in therapy together. He felt that the only way to be "restored to sanity" as the second step describes, is to do the footwork and be open to self-exploration.

As of this writing, Brian is six years clean and sober.

JEREMY'S STORY

Jeremy, on the other hand, struggled with looking beyond self. An altercation with his daughter led to Child Protective Services' (CPS) involvement. His wife was furious and so, to appease the family, he came to see me for eight employee assistance sessions. Jeremy is highly educated and works for a prominent nationwide company. The family altercation occurred when he punched a hole in his teenage daughter's bedroom door. Jeremy was inebriated and when his daughter responded to him in what he perceived as a disrespectful manner, he let loose on the door.

Jeremy was cooperative and articulate in treatment, but it was clear he did not want to evaluate the role of alcohol in his life and dismissed his fit of rage as harmless. He is a confident black man who felt he had overcome considerable discrimination to rise to the employment and academic level he had obtained. He truly believed drinking helped him cope with the "idiots" he had to interact with daily. He minimized the role both alcohol and anger played in the altercation, and as soon as the CPS case was closed and his wife calmed down, he artfully dropped out of treatment. Will he be back? I did my best to leave the door open.

Despite telling him information to the contrary, Jeremy truly believes that an alcoholic is an unemployed bum who lives on the street with little resources. He saw the issue as all or nothing and did not really accept that alcohol problems fall on a spectrum, and that treatment could be matched to that spectrum.

I can imagine what you're thinking here. I am relaying this to demonstrate that the most intelligent person, capable of sophisticated critical thinking skills, is still capable of distorting reality and factual information in order to protect their continued use of substances.

Perhaps Jeremy will be successful in cutting down his consumption and will not have to become abstinent and engage in recovery activities. However, from the family history he provided which was positive for alcoholism (father and uncles) and from discussions with family members (his wife and mother), it would appear that the odds are against him. Apparently, he has had significant alcohol-related problems over the years but has managed to skirt major consequences. I certainly wish him well and would assist him wholeheartedly should he return to treatment. At present, however, he doesn't believe he has a significant problem with either alcohol or anger and therefore reaching out for assistance and resources, in his view, is not necessary.

Before our sessions ended, I did speak with him at length about the advantages of utilizing a program such as Moderation Management to help him truly address moderation issues and provide a sense of accountability. Since he did not believe that abstinence was an appropriate goal, I thought this might be a good starting point to examine his relationship with alcohol. I also suggested he educate himself about the use of medication to assist with cravings should he decide in the future to try that option. I explained that there were FDA-approved medications in the United States that demonstrated effectiveness and could be helpful. I advised him to speak to his medical doctor or seek a referral to a psychiatrist with a practice in addiction medicine to discuss medication options should he be interested in doing so. He did not follow through with this recommendation during our time together but was genuinely appreciative of the information. He is now educated about these resources should he want to use them in the future.

Over the years many clients have returned to treatment to continue to address a substance abuse problem. Various issues and circumstances motivate people at different times. A person does not have to be ready to change. A willingness to explore the issue is an important first step. Often a client will discover what truly motivates them to change as they discuss their lives. Sometimes a client will leave treatment for a while and then return. I think it is important to be respectful and supportive of this process.

ADIA'S STORY

Recently, a female client returned to treatment after being away for four years. At the time Adia left treatment she had come off prescription medication but continued smoking pot and drinking. Over the course of her absence from therapy she lost her business, which included her place to live and a relationship with a person who was clean and sober and did not want to risk relapse being with her. Adia came to the realization that her chronic pot smoking and drinking was the major reason for the failure of her business and relationship. She quit both marijuana and alcohol, moved to a local mountain town and restarted her flower business.

She came to see me and said, "I really want to get clean and sober. I'm tired of being a failure with nothing to show for my life."

She drives a long distance weekly to attend our sessions and displays a motivation that was not there before. She has many demons to slay and a good deal of self-regulation to learn. Nevertheless, we are both optimistic!

2 - LOOKING BEYOND SELF

A SMART DOCTOR'S STORY

Back in the 1980s, I received a call from the local medical society. They were working with a physician and had hit a wall. He was a very talented and highly regarded doctor, but he was in advanced stages of alcoholism and would not quit. They had previously sent him to a long inpatient program in another state, and various psychiatrists had attempted to work with him. The society asked if I would see him and consult on the case. I agreed and we established a date and time. I have to admit, I don't have the best memory, but I remember the meeting with this physician with amazing clarity.

The building that housed my office was located near beautiful Balboa Park and when I returned that day from lunch, I thought one of the homeless men in the area had found his way into my office. Before me stood a man with disheveled clothing, a huge and swollen bruise on his forehead, and matted hair. It took me awhile to realize this was the doctor. I had seen him around the local hospitals for years and had known him to be a handsome, highly educated individual who had interns and nurses constantly flocking around him. He was brilliant and immensely respected. The man in my office did not resemble the man of my memory. Nevertheless, we began to talk.

My intervention was an utter failure. His intellectual defenses were impermeable. Sadly, I began to realize that he thought he could "think" his way out of the disease. Unfortunately, I could not help him understand the "Collective Wisdom" that the only way out was to "BEHAVE YOUR WAY OUT."

This gifted and talented man lost his medical license within six months of our meeting. He was dead within the year. That happened over 30 years ago, and I can still connect with the sadness I felt at his loss.

I often reflect on the clients with whom we know we did not succeed; they have perhaps taught us the most. In all sincerity I can say, "While I have never met a person not bright enough to successfully engage in recovery, I once did meet someone too smart."

ADULT CHILDREN OF ALCOHOLICS

Adult children of alcoholics are very susceptible to alcohol/drug abuse, not only because of potential genetic predisposition but because they may have lived in an environment fraught with stress, trauma, and uncertainty. These conditions can create great emotional pain and turmoil for these individuals and make them particularly vulnerable to the quick pain relief alcohol and drugs can provide. Tomorrow's alcoholics and addicts can be found among this population.

As these children grow into adulthood without addressing the trauma and or emotional distress they have experienced, the conditions are set for substance abuse. Individuals who recognize that they are problem drinking, abusing medication, or using other mood-altering substances to cope with their feelings and isolation should seek counseling support. It's hard to make that phone call or keep that first appointment. Many children of alcoholics have grown up to believe that it is futile to rely on anyone but themselves. Nevertheless, the act of reaching out is the first step to emotional freedom.

Counseling can help a person work through trauma and emotional pain so that they will not need to rely on a chemical fix to cope with life. Many individuals can avoid continued problematic use or serious substance

2 - LOOKING BEYOND SELF

use disorders by addressing these issues early and effectively. Community 12-step support groups such as Adult Children of Alcoholics/Dysfunctional Families can provide welcome fellowship and support to help heal the abuse, shame, trauma, and abandonment often experienced in dysfunctional families [3].

Adult children of alcoholics often need resources and assistance to heal the past and manage very real emotional pain. This point was made to me in the most poignant way in 1995.

SAPPORO JAPAN

Over the years, I have traveled to Japan to conduct workshops and training seminars on the treatment of substance abuse for social workers and other treatment professionals. On various occasions, I have also provided public seminars on related topics including adult children of alcoholics.

In 1995, I agreed to travel to northern Japan to provide training at a hospital facility in Sapporo. I agreed to travel in the dead of winter because Sapporo hosts an amazing ice festival annually in February. It is a true wonder to behold. Huge scenes are carved from ice. Buildings, cartoon characters, and intricate sculptures occupy several streets in this wondrous festival.

My hosts asked if I would also do a public lecture on adult children of alcoholics. At the time, there were few resources or translated books available and they wanted to provide an opportunity for the public to receive some information. I agreed, and my tour translator was also retained to provide the translation. I worked up a presentation and gave it to the translator so that she could familiarize herself with the content. As fate would have it, there was a significant storm on the day of the presentation. While Sapporo is accustomed to difficult winter weather conditions, this storm was particularly intense. I felt very badly for my hosts. They had gone to considerable expense to secure an auditorium, the translator, materials, and advertising. I vividly remember looking through my hotel window thinking I would be lucky if a handful of people attended, and fully expected them to cancel the event.

When the time arrived, I made my way to the auditorium near my hotel. The weather continued to remain terrible. When I walked into the entrance, I was never as surprised in my life. The auditorium was packed with people. Every seat was taken and people lined the walls. Please believe me when I say that the collective pain in that room was palpable. I knew immediately that my academic presentation would not be adequate. I turned to my translator and said, "Forget the presentation, can you follow me?" She smiled and said, "Don't worry, we have worked together a long time now, I will be able to follow you."

I began to speak to the audience and acknowledged the pain and emotional distress that so many children of alcoholics experience. I recognized that the audience members felt this pain intensely and not only needed information, but more importantly, hope and encouragement that they were not alone. I spoke for over two hours. I took questions from the audience. The most frequently asked question stated in a variety of ways was basically "Will I ever feel better?"

I have spoken extensively over the years but never has an engagement been such a profound experience. It made me realize that adult children of alcoholics are

2 - LOOKING BEYOND SELF

everywhere in the world. Many suffer in silence and never share their pain nor access resources to help them heal. Since 1995, Japan, as well as other countries in the world, has benefited from information available on the internet and the translation of many fine books and articles on the subject. In addition, I know that treatment professionals in Japan are working diligently to address the needs of this population. As I stated earlier, this population is vulnerable to excessive substance use. Providing counseling services, self-help support, and other resources will contribute significantly toward breaking the cycle of alcoholism in families.

A final note. On the day I was leaving Sapporo, as I was waiting at the airport terminal, a young man who had attended my lecture approached me. Apparently, he had learned of the day I was leaving and went to the airport searching for me in the various departure lounges. I spoke with him until it was time for the plane to depart. He was in a tremendous amount of emotional pain and appeared to be suffering from depression. He was desperate to know if he would ever feel safe and "normal." I did my best to comfort him, and my hosts agreed to ensure that they would connect him to treatment resources. It was clear he needed a medication evaluation and that was something that could be accomplished quickly. We hugged as I departed. Today, I cannot recall his face, but I can still recall his profound pain. I truly hope he found assistance and was able to find the emotional healing he so desperately sought.

FURTHER INFORMATION

MODERATION MANAGEMENT: MM

"Moderation Management (MM) is a behavioral change program and national support group network for people concerned about their drinking and who desire to make positive lifestyle changes [4]."

According to MM literature, 30 percent of their members go on to abstinence-based programs. MM literature also asserts that outcome studies indicate that professional programs offering both moderation and abstinence have higher success rates than those that offer abstinence-only. MM contends that clients tend to self-select the behavior change options which will work best for them [4].

I would add a caveat to that notion. Individuals in early stages of substance use disorder tend to still retain the cognitive functioning that will support healthy and rational decision-making. However, individuals in latter stages of addiction have been psychologically compromised and rational decision-making may not be possible. MM would be an option to consider for those in the very early (mild) stages of substance use disorder or problematic drinking.

Audrey Kishline founded Moderation Management. In her struggle with alcohol, she believed she could moderate her drinking utilizing cognitive-behavioral principles. In 1994, she founded Moderation Management as an organization for non-dependent problem drinkers to help them maintain the moderate consumption of alcohol [5][6].

In January 2000, Ms. Kishline posted a message to the MM Membership "stating she had concluded that her best drinking goal was abstinence and that she would begin attending A.A., and Women for Sobriety meetings while continuing to support Moderation Management for others [5][6]." In March 2000, Audrey Kishline, in a state of intoxication, drove her truck in the wrong direction down a highway. She "hit another vehicle head-on, killing its two passengers (a father and his 12-year-old daughter) [5]." Ms. Kishline was sentenced to prison for this tragic collision. She was released in August 2003 after serving 3.5 years of a 4.5-year sentence [5].

This was a sad and heartbreaking situation. Apparently, Ms. Kishline recognized that she could not properly moderate her alcohol consumption and determined she needed to change to an abstinence-based lifestyle. Within weeks of that decision, she drank and drove, ending two precious lives. Nothing underscores the risks associated with attempted moderation management of an alcohol problem more than the above story.

There is definite risk associated with the decision and it is important to consider your options carefully. However, this should not negate the thousands of individuals who have been successful with this program or other moderation efforts. Audrey Kishline gave the community an important component to the substance abuse treatment continuum. Her contribution was worthy and significant.

Sadly, it did not work for her. In 2014, Ms. Kishline, apparently unable to cope and find emotional relief, killed herself [6].

Author Amy Girvan stated the following in an article in 2015: "In the years since her death (Ms. Kishline), Moderation Management has had something of a resurgence, bolstered by the launch of the U.S. National Institute of Health's Rethinking Drinking Program and a 2014 report from the Center of Disease Control, calling out 'excessive drinking' as something both independent of alcohol dependence and a major public health issue that is not being adequately addressed by currently available tools and programs [7]."

Today, experts recognize Moderation Management as an evidenced-based program. It is listed on SAMHSA's National Registry of Evidenced-based Programs and Practices [8].

The Moderation Management website lists "Nine Steps Toward Moderation and Positive Lifestyle Change [9]." They point out that according to NIAAA and other independent researchers, there are four times as many problem drinkers as alcoholics in this country. Moderation Management offers a helpful and much-needed service for beginning-stage problem drinkers [4].

The Moderation Management "Nine Steps Toward Moderation and Positive Lifestyle Changes" [9]:

1. Attend meetings or on-line groups and learn about the program of Moderation Management.
2. Abstain from alcoholic beverages for 30 days and complete steps three through six during this time. +++
3. Examine how drinking has affected your life.
4. Write down your life priorities.
5. Take a look at how much, how often, and under what circumstances you have been drinking.
6. Learn the MM guidelines and limits for moderate drinking.

7. Set moderate drinking limits and start weekly "small steps" toward balance and moderation in other areas of your life.
8. Review your progress and update your goals.
9. Continue to make positive lifestyle changes and attend meetings whenever you need ongoing support or would like to help newcomers.

+++ If you have any concerns about abstaining from alcohol in regard to detoxification, consult with your medical doctor first.

If you would like to attempt to manage your drinking, and would welcome assistance and fellowship in doing so, this program might prove invaluable. I would suggest that, in addition to practicing the nine steps of the program, also consider the themes of the PDMT Model described in this book as you consider the self-examination, accountability, and self-regulation components of lifestyle management [1].

REFERENCE LIST

[1] L.G. DiStefano, LCSW and M. Hohman, Ph.D., *The Paradigm Developmental Model of Treatment: A Clinical Guide for Counselors Working with Substance Abusers and the Chemically Dependent.* San Diego, CA: Montezuma Publishing, 2010.

[2] Alcoholics Anonymous World Services, Inc. (2016, Aug.). *The Twelve Steps of Alcoholics Anonymous* [Online]. Available: http://www.aa.org/assets/en_US/smf-121_en.pdf

[3] Adult Children of Alcoholics World Service Organization, Inc. (2017). *Welcome to Adult Children*

of Alcoholics/Dysfunctional Families [Online]. Available: www.adultchildren.org

[4] Moderation Management. (2017). *What is Moderation Management?* [Online]. Available: www.moderation.org/about_mm/whatismm.html

[5] Wikipedia. (2017, Jun. 29). *Moderation Management in Wikipedia, the Free Encyclopedia* [Online]. Available: https://en.wikipedia.org/w/index.php?title=Moderation_Management&oldid=788167743

[6] R. Walker. (2015, Jan.). *Remembering Audrey Kishline, the Founder of Moderation Management.* [Online]. Available: https://www.thefix.com/content/remembering-audrey-kishline

[7] A. Girvan (2015, Mar. 15) *The Next AA? Welcome to Moderation Management, Where Abstinence from Alcohol Isn't the Answer* [Online]. Available: https://www.theguardian.com/society/2015/mar/16/the-next-aa-moderation-management-abstinence-alcohol-isnt-the-answer

[8] NREPP, SAMHSA's National Registry of Evidence-based Programs and Practices (2016, Jan. 07). *Moderate Drinking.com and Moderation Management* [Online]. Available: http://legacy.nreppadmin.net/ViewIntervention.aspx?id=212

[9] Moderation Management (2017) *Nine Steps toward Moderation Management and Positive Lifestyle Changes* [Online]. Available: http://moderation.org/meetings/readings.html

CHAPTER 3

THEME 3
LETTING GO

The third theme of the PDMT Model is Letting Go [1]. It is an alternative secular interpretation of the third A.A. step: "Made a decision to turn our will and our lives over to the care of God as we understood him [2]."

From a cognitive perspective, Letting Go refers to a willingness to release preconceptions in the way we think and old ways of doing things. This theme works hand in hand with Theme #2: Looking Beyond Self [1].

Imagine you decide to invest your retirement savings. You go to a highly regarded company and meet with an experienced licensed advisor. At this point, you have looked beyond yourself for help. The advisor gives you several recommendations based on sound research and encourages you to check it out and get a second opinion. Nevertheless, you decide that none of the recommendations are valuable. You also don't want to obtain a second opinion. You just want to do it yourself regardless of the fact you have no experience in this area. In this scenario, your reaction may be based on the fact that you can't let go of your distrust in others. Despite vetting this financial company carefully, you cannot take the step of putting your trust in their hands.

In many areas of life, we may replicate this reaction. You hire a contractor to help you renovate your home and then disregard a number of sound recommendations. A medical doctor may make a recommendation about a lifestyle change that you ignore. Unfortunately, when it comes to recovery, many ignored recommendations could be lifesaving.

CHILDREN OF ALCOHOLICS

As noted in the previous chapter, many problem abusers, alcoholics, and addicts are children of alcoholics

3 - LETTING GO

and addicts. For many years I ran group therapy sessions in a chemical dependency program and asked the question, "How many people have or had a parent or grandparent with an alcohol/drug problem?" Invariably at least 60 percent of the group would raise their hands.

This is important information. The lessons learned in childhood growing up in a family where alcohol/drugs are a central factor can be significant. For example, to survive a childhood with an alcoholic mother, children must quickly learn to take care of themselves. They can't rely on mom to pack lunch or go to a school appointment or event. They sadly learn to only count on themselves. These children survive childhood by over developing their sense of self-reliance.

Now fast forward to adulthood. These same individuals become confused when their spouses state, "You're shutting me out, you don't let me help." It is not hard to see from where that comes. Now, as adults, these individuals have difficulty trusting that others will come through for them or that advice can be in their best interest. These reactions can cause considerable problems in a marriage and often lead to separation and divorce. We often see these dynamics in marriage counseling. Now, further complicate the issue by adding a problem with alcohol or other drugs.

The problem abuser, alcoholic/addict who grows up in a family system that created distrust and disengagement, may find it difficult to work with a counselor or A.A. sponsor. In therapy, it is important to acknowledge that the "over self-reliance" did in fact, help them survive their childhood. Without that focus, life would have been much more complicated and perhaps disastrous. Now however, as an adult, they will need to develop a new set of skills to thrive and support their resiliencies. They will need to learn the value of "interdependence" and the benefits that come from the "Collective Wisdom" of the recovery community. But it's hard to let go and trust the council of others when you have only depended on yourself.

Another dynamic further complicates this issue.

THE NEGATIVE COMMITTEE

The term "negative committee" has been used in the recovery community for many years. It describes the negative mental self-talk that goes on in our heads. In cognitive-behavioral therapy, we call these thoughts distorted or inaccurate automatic thoughts [3]. The purpose of the "negative committee" is clear: to get a person to break their commitments and or abstinence and begin abusing alcohol/drugs again. The "negative committee" is insidious. It figures out where you are emotionally vulnerable and continually plays on those issues. It is the driver behind the often-subconscious self-sabotage that people endure.

COGNITIVE SCHEMAS

In psychology, we also have the term "schema." A schema represents a deep core belief about self. Some common schemas are rooted in the issues of abandonment, mistrust, emotional deprivation, alienation, incompetence, pessimism, enmeshment, and entitlement [4].

A schema functions as a framework in our brain to organize and interpret information. If a person has a core belief that they are incompetent, they will filter

3 - LETTING GO

information/feedback from the world to support that negative belief.

Let's suppose a person is a handyman. They do several local jobs and get reviews from customers. Let's say there are ten reviews. Five are excellent, four are good, and one is poor. That individual will screen out most of the positive feedback and focus on the one poor review to help support their belief that they are incompetent. While this is a simplistic example, it illustrates the point. An individual will filter—in countless and improbable ways—their experiences and the feedback they receive to support whatever their negative schema is. Remember a schema defies logic or reason. Working with a counselor/therapist with the PDMT model can be very helpful with these types of issues. As a person works through the themes of the PDMT Model, they have an opportunity to identify and change the filter they are using to interpret the events of life.

You often hear in the community the "Collective Wisdom" that "IT'S NOT A DRINKING PROBLEM, IT'S A LIVING PROBLEM." If all that was necessary was abstinence, why would so many people be attending various forms of self-help many years into abstinence? The reason is, it takes a lot of work to address the underlying schemas that influence our mental filters. The more we can clean the filter and change our core beliefs about self, the stronger and more long-lasting recovery can be.

The final paradigm of the PDMT model is "Transformation [1]." This word truly personifies the mental and behavioral changes that a person experiences in creating a lasting recovery. Often in recovery, individuals relapse because they have not changed or "let go" of a behavior or core belief that negatively impacts them.

SAMANTHA'S STORY

I will tell you upfront that this story broke my heart. Sammy came into therapy with three years of recovery. She was in her mid-thirties and did battle with heroin, prescription meds, and alcohol. She had gone through an inpatient treatment program and regularly attended Narcotics Anonymous. On the advice of her sponsor, she came into treatment. Over the course of the next two years, Sammy worked very hard. She decided she wanted to become a substance abuse counselor and attended a program for a certificate at a local college.

Samantha was insightful, empathic, and hard working. Her gains in therapy were significant. It became clear however that she had one problem of which she could not let go.

Sammy supported herself financially by prostitution; she was a high-priced call girl for more than a decade. After becoming clean and sober, her business improved a great deal, and she was able to save considerable money. However, the dissonance between the ethics of her self-help program and her employment choice became greater as her recovery grew. Initially she thought that becoming a counselor would provide a new career path, but she soon learned how poorly paid alcohol counselors were. Nevertheless, she had many colleagues who lived on the wages provided by alcohol and drug counseling, and she knew she could manage.

Sammy had a core schema of emotional deprivation. On some level, her recurring clientele provided the attention, connection, and acceptance, if

3 - LETTING GO

not the love, she craved. Sammy knew that her behavior put her at risk, but she remained reluctant to close the business. She ended treatment after two years. She now had five years of recovery and obtained a job as an AOD Counselor at a local facility. She said she wanted to leave the call girl business within the year.

About two years later I received a call from Sammy asking to see me. When she arrived for the appointment, I noticed something different about her but could not figure out what it was. She told me that she became so angry at her dog that she almost kicked him. This frightened her deeply as she adored her animal and always treated him well. She said she had increased her meeting attendance and was talking more regularly with her sponsor but was having urges to shoot heroin for the first time in years.

I finally asked her what was different about her. She smiled proudly and stated, "I had a face lift; he did a great job didn't he?" I soon learned that she had not given up her call girl business and was scared of the younger competition in town. She had the facelift to help mask her age.

Suddenly, a bell went off in my head. She had had I.V. sedation anesthesia with the operation and took Percocet briefly and as prescribed post-surgery, followed by Tylenol. She explained that she had taken the medication strictly as prescribed. Nevertheless, she apparently minimized her addiction to the doctor, and irritability and cravings soon followed. I suggested she resume individual treatment or enter an outpatient treatment program for additional support.

She did not want to jeopardize her job by entering rehab, nor did she want to resume regular counseling with me. She felt that a closer working relationship with her sponsor would be helpful. I suspected that she realized in counseling we would at some point address her continued prostitution and she still was not ready to go there.

About 18 months later I ran into Sammy at a store. The change was shocking; she looked terrible. The always immaculately groomed woman was disheveled and gaunt. She admitted to me that she had relapsed, but this time she became involved with something new to her: crack cocaine. My heart dropped when she told me this. She had lost her counseling job, and most of her rich clientele were long gone. She had become a street prostitute with little money. I told her to see me and I would help her get into a county treatment program. I scheduled her an appointment for the following day and told her not to worry about payment, that we could work that out. She never came and I never heard from her again.

Sammy is one of the souls that I keep in my prayers nightly. I hope that she has found her way back to recovery, but my instincts tell me she has not. Had she let go of her prostitution business and addressed the deeper therapy topic of confronting her schema of emotional deprivation around the issues of psychological nurturance, love, attention, and connection, her recovery might have strengthened. While she was able to let go of drugs for a significant period, she was not able to "let go" of an insatiable need for attention and acceptance that prostitution provided.

I believe this contributed to the risky decision of having elective surgery and what the community refers to as "waking the sleeping tiger." The anesthesia and

Percocet most likely stimulated her brain chemistry and her response was to do too little, too late. Crack cocaine is perhaps the most addictive substance and I know Sammy had to have known that. I think Sammy knew when she relapsed that she was not coming back. She just could not let go and trust a new way of life.

I have to conclude by saying that not only have we most likely lost Sammy to her addiction, but sadly, in addition, so many people are denied the help and support she could have provided as an active member of the recovery community. The "Collective Wisdom" here is that "IN RELAPSE PEOPLE MAY NOT COME BACK" and we lose many incredibly talented and wonderful people to this disease. If you're in recovery, never underestimate the ability of the disease to come roaring back.

ESTELLA'S STORY

Some people are able to "let go" despite the emotional pain and associated losses. Estella came to me seeking therapy upon a recommendation from a friend in the program. At one point in her recovery history she had been clean for ten years. She believed in the A.A. program, but continually relapsed over the preceding five years. Her husband Carl, a prominent businessman, had a serious alcohol dependency. He not only refused counseling or treatment but constantly sabotaged Estella's attempts to remain sober. Estella was a committed wife and educated woman. Her parents came from Latin America to give her greater opportunities and she thrived here.

After obtaining advanced degrees, she took a job with the Internal Revenue Service (IRS) and worked her way up the ladder. She created a beautiful home, had many long-time friends, and was devoted to her two stepchildren. Nevertheless, Carl's drinking was becoming untenable. One day her sponsor confronted her and told her "You can't stay sober living with Carl." Instantly, she knew this was true. With a courage that is rare, she asked her agency for a transfer to California and came to San Diego. She left her home of 20 years, her friends, and associates, and decided she needed to be away and start focusing on herself.

When I met Estella, she was grieving the loss of her marriage and all that was familiar. She rented a house in a nearby community and with the exception of her dog and phone support, she was alone.

The holidays that year were very painful for her, and agreeing to my recommendation she began using Antabuse during this difficult period. The divorce was exceptionally nasty and disappointing. Her requests appeared very reasonable and generous, but her husband was angry and felt abandoned. Even her stepchildren felt they had to take sides and support their father, although his serious drinking problem was evident for all to see. Estella lost a good deal in the divorce. She smartly understood that possessions could be replaced and money could be earned anew, but recovery was essential to having a life. So she let go of the possessions, money, and relationships, and more importantly, over time she "let go" of her resentments and forgave Carl (more on that later).

Today Estella is enjoying the gifts of her recovery. She has made new friends, rents a lovely condo, and is thriving at work. Since her divorce, she dates occasionally and recently saw a childhood boyfriend when he came into town. There may be more to that story.

CORE BELIEFS

Estella had the advantage of good core beliefs about herself. She knew she was smart and attractive. She felt loved and nurtured during her childhood. Even though there was alcoholism in the family history (grandparent), it did not directly affect her growing up. This emotional stability was a great asset in getting through the tough times.

Although Estella experienced searing pain and loss, her "negative committee" was manageable. Most often it would make her feel guilty for breaking her marriage vows and leaving her husband. When these bouts of guilt occurred, and they frequently did at first, she would call her sponsor or come in for a session.

Estella recognized an important recovery concept that has become part of the "Collective Wisdom," "DON'T FIGHT A NEGATIVE THOUGHT WITH ONLY A POSITIVE THOUGHT, BECAUSE A POSITIVE THOUGHT MIGHT NOT BE STRONG ENOUGH. FIGHT A NEGATIVE THOUGHT WITH A POSITIVE ACTION!"

Whenever Estella would start to hear the negative committee, she would respond with a positive action, e.g., phone call, counseling session, meeting, or something similar. These responses saved her during that first difficult year of separation. In therapy Estella grew in her strengths and learned to manage her vulnerabilities.

I hear from Estella periodically. She leaves lovely voice messages and holiday greetings. She now sponsors others in her program. "Passing it on" is another fundamental ingredient for ongoing success.

FURTHER INFORMATION

Letting go of our negative conceptions about medication for alcohol and substance use disorders is essential. Despite a clear body of research both in the United States and Europe that several FDA-approved medications can contribute significantly to the treatment of moderate to severe alcohol use disorders, there continues to be a hesitancy for treatment programs, physicians, and specialists to embrace these additional tools.

Author Gabrielle Glaser asks a critical question in an article she wrote in the *Atlantic Monthly*. In discussing individuals who have not managed to achieve sobriety she asks, "Why do we assume they failed the program, rather than the program failed them?" While I do not agree with all aspects of her article, she makes some critical points to consider [5].

According to another article in *Frontiers in Psychiatry*, the National Institute of Alcohol Abuse and Alcoholism (NIAAA) recommends that facilities consider medication for patients with alcohol dependence, also known as severe alcohol use disorder. Nevertheless, they cite federal data from substance abuse treatment facilities across the United States (2013) that reveals only 17 to 19 percent of these facilities prescribe FDA-approved medications for alcohol use disorders [6].

We now recognize that alcohol problems fall on a spectrum and that not one approach works for every individual. We need to consider more individualized treatment options. Medication should be regarded as an important element of treatment for appropriate cases.

American neuroscientist John Sinclair spent decades in Finland researching alcohol and the brain, working with drugs that block opiate receptors. Subsequent research found that an opioid antagonist called naltrexone was safe and effective for humans.

Sinclair opened several private clinics in Finland. He worked with treatment personnel and suggested prescribing naltrexone for patients to take an hour before drinking. It proved to be effective. Patients reported that their cravings subsided and they regained greater control over their consumption. Numerous clinical trials have confirmed similar results. In 2001 Sinclair reported a 78 percent success rate in helping patients reduce their drinking. That was 16 years ago.

Naltrexone is currently used in the United States, with patients routinely instructed to avoid alcohol altogether, whereas in Finland and other countries they are instructed to take the drug anytime they plan to drink. Despite intense disagreement as to which approach is better, both have been proven to work [6].

While it is difficult to scientifically evaluate the effectiveness of 12-step programs and other support groups due to their structure and anonymous membership, it is not difficult to evaluate the effectiveness of medication. We already have the research that proves it can be of significant help to many individuals and an important component to treatment. According to author Gabrielle Glaser, "unfortunately less than one percent of people treated for alcohol problems in the United States are prescribed naltrexone or any other drug shown to help control drinking [5]."

Here is a brief review of the medications available in the United States. I strongly urge any interested individual to go online and review the literature and have a serious discussion with your medical doctor or ask for a referral to speak with a psychiatrist who specializes in addiction medicine. Adding medication to your treatment regime could be a game changer!

MEDICATIONS FOR TREATMENT OF ALCOHOL USE DISORDERS

ACAMPROSATE (CAMPRAL)

"...used along with counseling and social support to help people who have stopped drinking large amounts of alcohol (alcoholism) to avoid drinking alcohol again [7]."

It helps ease cravings. It works by helping the brains of people who have consumed large amounts of alcohol to function properly again. It does not prevent withdrawal symptoms associated with the abrupt cessation of alcohol use. It also has not been shown to work in people who have not stopped drinking. Please note that this medication has been used in Europe for over 20 years before it became approved in the United States. It's important to learn and understand the various side effects of this medication and make an informed choice [7].

According to the Substance Abuse and Mental Health Services Administration (SAMHSA), acamprosate is in the top three of evidenced-based treatment approaches [8].

DISULFIRAM (ANTABUSE)

Disulfiram was the first medication available to assist with alcohol dependence [9]. When a person taking disulfiram ingests alcohol, severe, unpleasant, physical reactions occur including vomiting, facial flushing, nausea, and other serious symptoms. This is an aversion medicine whose effectiveness depends on the person's reluctance to suffer the aversive effects of drinking while on this medication [10]. Over the years I have seen great success with Antabuse as well as complete failure. This medication is a treatment tool: motivation is the key. If a person sincerely wants assistance with remaining sober, and has some mechanism in place for accountability, this can be a very effective component to their treatment.

NALTREXONE (AN OPIOID ANTAGONIST)

This medication blocks opioid receptors leading to reductions in cravings and in the reinforcing effects of alcohol. Vivitrol is an injectable naltrexone [9][13].

Please note: clients with liver damage usually cannot use either naltrexone or disulfiram. However, because acamprosate is not metabolized in the liver, clients with liver damage can usually take the medication. Discuss these issues with your medical doctor [8].

MEDICATIONS FOR TREATMENT OF SUBSTANCE USE DISORDERS

BUPRENORPHINE

This medication reduces or eliminates opioid withdrawal symptoms, including drug cravings, without producing the 'high' or dangerous side effects of heroin and other opioids [11]. It does this by both activating and blocking opioid receptors in the brain. There is a stand-alone formulation called Subutex and a combination formulation called Suboxone. The combination is designed to deter abuse of the medication by causing a withdrawal reaction if it is intravenously injected [11]. Physicians with special certification may provide office-based buprenorphine treatment for detoxification and or maintenance therapy.

METHADONE

This medication has been around for many years and has a controversial history. It prevents withdrawal symptoms and reduces craving in opioid addicted individuals by activating opioid receptors in the brain [12]. This medication is available in specially licensed methadone treatment programs. The quality of these treatment programs can vary but some are excellent and provide a much-needed resource.

NALTREXONE

In addition to using this medication for alcohol use disorders, it is approved for the prevention of relapse in adult patients following complete detoxification from opioids. Vivitrol is also used for this purpose [13].

NALOXONE (NARCAN)

This is a nasal spray medicine used for emergency treatment of known or suspected opioid overdose. It temporarily reverses the effects of opioid medicines [14].

MEDICATIONS FOR NICOTINE USE DISORDERS

BUPROPION (ZYBAN)

This medication reduces nicotine cravings and withdrawal symptoms [15][17].

NICOTINE REPLACEMENT THERAPY (NRT)

Helps smokers wean off cigarettes by activating nicotinic receptors in the brain [16][17].

VARENICLINE (CHANTIX)

This medication reduces nicotine cravings and withdrawal in adult smokers by mildly stimulating nicotinic receptors in the brain. [17].

> **IN SUMMARY**
>
> Our increasing knowledge of alcohol and other drugs' neurobiological effects on the brain have led to the development of well-researched pharmacotherapies that should be seriously considered when determining treatment options. Unfortunately, the medical community underutilizes medications for substance use disorders. Clients themselves, and their advocates, may have to take the lead when discussing medication options with their treatment providers. A medication regime, a social support network, and cognitive-behavioral/motivational counseling can create a powerful response to these disorders.

REFERENCE LIST

[1] L.G. DiStefano, LCSW and M. Hohman, Ph.D., *The Paradigm Developmental Model of Treatment: A Clinical Guide for Counselors Working with Substance Abusers and the Chemically Dependent*. San Diego, CA: Montezuma Publishing, 2010.

[2]   Alcoholics Anonymous World Services, Inc. (2016, Aug.). *The Twelve Steps of Alcoholics Anonymous* [Online]. Available: http://www.aa.org/assets/en_US/smf-121en.pdf

[3]   P. Nugent, M.S. (2013, Apr.) "Automatic Thoughts," in *PsychologyDictionary.org* [Online]. Available: https://psychologydictionary.org/automatic-thoughts/

[4]   M. Cameron. *Schema Therapy* [Online]. Available: http://cognitivetherapy.me.uk/schema_therapy.htm

[5]   Gabrielle Glaser. (2015, Apr.) *The Irrationality of Alcoholics Anonymous* [Online]. Available: https://www.theatlantic.com/magazine/archive/2015/04/the-irrationality-of-alcoholics-anonymous/386255/?utm_source=atlfb

[6]   C. Ponce Martinez et al. (2016, Nov.) "Pharmacotherapy for alcohol use disorders: Physicians perceptions and practices," *Frontiers in Psychiatry*. vol. 7, p.182. [Online] Available: https://www.frontiersin.org/articles/10.3389/fpsyt.2016.00182/full

[7]   American Society of Health-System Pharmacists, Inc., and National Institute of Health: U.S. National Library of Medicine: MedlinePlus. (2016, May). *Acamprosate* [Online]. Available: https://medlineplus.gov/druginfo/meds/a604028.html

[8]   Center for Substance Abuse Treatment. "Acamprosate: A new medication for alcohol use disorder," *Substance Abuse Treatment Advisory*, volume 4, no. 1, Fall, 2005.

[9]   NIH: National Institute on Alcohol Abuse and Alcoholism. *Medications Development Program* [Online]. Available: https://www.niaaa.nih.gov/research/major-initiatives/medications-Development-program

[10] NetDoctor. (2013, Nov.) *Antabuse (Disulfiram)* [Online]. Available: http://www.netdoctor.co.uk/medicines/brain-and-nervous-system/a6217/antabuse-disulfiram/

[11] The National Alliance of Advocates for Buprenorphine Treatment. *What Exactly is Buprenorphine?* [Online]. Available: https://www.naabt.org/faq_answers.cfm?ID=2

[12] Substance Abuse and Mental Health Services Administration. (2015, Sept. 28). *Medication Assisted Treatment: Methadone* [Online]. Available: https://www.samhsa.gov/medication-assisted-treatment/treatment/methadone

[13] Substance Abuse and Mental Health Services Administration. (2016, Sept. 12). *Medication Assisted Treatment: Naltrexone* [Online]. Available: https://www.samhsa.gov/medication-assisted-treatment/treatment/naltrexone

[14] Drugs.com. (2017, June). *Narcan* [Online]. Available: https://www.drugs.com/pro/narcan.html

[15] Drugs.com. (2017, May). *Zyban* [Online]. Available: https://www.drugs.com/zyban.html

[16] R. Hefflinger, Pharm.D. (2013, Dec.). *Science of Nicotine Replacement Therapy and E-cigarettes* [Online]. Available: http://cdhd.idaho.gov/pdfs/cd/Roger_Hefflinger_slides_TFIA%2012.09.13.pdf

[17] NIH National Institute of Drug Abuse. (2012, Dec.). *Principles of Drug Addiction Treatment: A Research-Based Guide (Third Edition) - Varenicline (Chantix®)* [Online]. Available: https://www.drugabuse.gov/publications/principles-drug-addiction-treatment-research-based-guide-third-edition/evidence-based-approaches-to-drug-addiction-treatment/pharmacotherapi-0

PARADIGM CHANGE

PARADIGM 2
TAKING RESPONSIBILITY

PARADIGM CHANGE

CHAPTER 4

THEME 4
SELF-EXAMINATION

PARADIGM 2: TAKING RESPONSIBILITY

The fourth theme of the PDMT Model is Self-Examination. This theme ushers in the beginning of Paradigm 2, "Taking Responsibility." There are five themes in this paradigm cluster. Paradigm 2 occurs when an individual begins a process of abstinence and wants to engage in recovery. The focus of this cluster is self-examination and taking responsibility for one's choices. The willingness and action to change behaviorally are essential to this paradigm process. By working through the second paradigm, individuals become engaged and accountable and grow in their empathy and compassion. An important focus for clients is relapse prevention planning and an understanding of their self-sabotaging behaviors, strengths, and resiliencies. Co-occurring disorders need to be identified and dual recovery treatment established as early as possible. This paradigm provides an opportunity for individuals to learn the fundamentals of recovery and valuable tools and strategies necessary for long-term success [1].

THEME 4: SELF-EXAMINATION

When someone starts counseling, they begin a process of reflection and self-examination. Working in therapy on this theme however, is a very specific process that occurs in earnest after an individual has begun sobriety and has obtained some initial stability and mental clarity. Those that have successfully stabilized with a moderation approach can also benefit from this work.

A.A.'s fourth step reads, "Made a searching and fearless moral inventory of ourselves [2]." Individuals who engage in A.A. work on this step with their program

4 - SELF-EXAMINATION

sponsors. In counseling, the work on these and related issues can go to a deeper level and reveal lifelong patterns tied to core beliefs about self. This is an important process, as self-understanding and the ability to identify and address self-defeating behaviors, schemas, and irrational thinking is essential to growth and change.

Many of my clients involved in A.A. have devoted considerable time identifying "character defects" and other emotional liabilities, which is certainly an important undertaking. However, I have been struck by how little real attention my clients paid to identifying their strengths and resiliencies before engaging in therapy.

A useful self-examination is an ongoing process that strikes a balance between identifying and addressing liabilities and identifying and supporting one's strengths and resiliencies. I highly recommend engaging in counseling if you discover that you have significant patterns of self-sabotage. If you are in A.A. working the fourth step with a sponsor, that's an important beginning.

However, if you are the child of an alcoholic, have experienced trauma, have had a particularly difficult childhood, or have created serious problems for yourself by your emotional/behavioral responses to life events, further professional assistance may be needed. I believe counseling with an experienced cognitive-behavioral therapist who works with substance use disorders can be extremely helpful in assisting you with a thorough and well-balanced self-examination.

Once you have initiated abstinence and your head has cleared, the process of self-examination will set the stage for your ongoing recovery. It is also an important reflective process for those who have successfully moderated their drinking: it's the foundation for all that comes next. This knowledge is essential to accomplishing your life goals. It will be painful at times to admit personal flaws, explore feelings of shame, and discuss behaviors of which you are not proud. However, it is also enlightening to recognize the strengths that have helped you survive and how you can effectively use those resiliencies to thrive in recovery. If you are utilizing another type of support group, e.g., SMART Recovery, Secular Organization for Sobriety, or a faith-based program, adding cognitive-behavioral counseling to your recovery efforts could be very beneficial.

THEIR STORIES CONTINUE...

Let's look at the self-examination issues of several clients I have already discussed.

RAY'S SELF-EXAMINATION

Ray addressed his self-examination over the course of several years as his tolerance for handling emotional pain grew. His schema was one of "defectiveness and shame." His mother's addiction and life of prostitution made Ray's childhood extremely difficult. He remembered many evenings when he had to stay away from home. Ray had to fend for himself for as long as he could remember. He did not feel valued or loved.

From an early age, Ray believed that he was the problem. At school, he saw the affection and involvement of other kids with their parents, and he felt, on a profound level, that he was unlovable. During many years of his marriage, he would often self-sabotage the relationship, believing that he was inadequate and his wife would eventually leave him. His inability to stop drinking, despite numerous adverse consequences, further reinforced his shame.

It was hard for Ray to identify his strengths, and his wife was instrumental in this reflection. She pointed out that the family always lived free of financial worry due to Ray's efforts and systematic savings. As time passed, being clean and sober, he was able to acknowledge that folks gravitated toward him and that others valued his humor and good will.

Ray was very kind and empathic, which led him to host and organize countless holiday gatherings for newcomers in the program. This increased his self-esteem and self-respect. His tolerance for criticism also grew as Ray began to see more gray, and less black and white, in his view of the world.

We built on Ray's strengths and helped him emotionally understand why, as a small child, he would be wounded by his mother's self-involvement and rejecting behavior. His own recovery as well as the struggle of friends in the program helped Ray to understand his mother's addiction with greater insight and empathy. A pivotal moment of healing occurred when he went to his mother's grave and forgave her. We will discuss this in greater detail later, but suffice it to say, forgiveness is a powerful response that allows for healing and peace.

CLAUDE'S SELF-EXAMINATION

Claude is the elderly client with a long history of adverse consequences to his drinking. He was able to identify pride as a flaw in his character that contributed significantly to his dysfunction. In between the serious consequences, Claude functioned well enough to pacify his wife and family. He was an intellectual and consistently minimized the problems associated with his use. Over time Claude was able to acknowledge an excessively high opinion of himself and his importance. To his credit, Claude worked hard to counter these narcissistic tendencies and develop humility and gratitude. He recognized that his life was spared on numerous occasions and that it was his turn to give back. Claude preferred the SMART Recovery program for fellowship and attended faithfully. As an atheist, he did not believe in a higher power, but he felt that there was much to be grateful for and that he had more than his share of luck.

Claude had exceptional strengths. He had a keen intellect and innate curiosity. He loved various cultures, and travel in sobriety became very meaningful to him. Claude is resilient, and he has thrived in his sobriety. His major regret is that it took so many years to become clean and sober.

SCOTT'S SELF-EXAMINATION

Scott continues to struggle with his alcoholism. He attempts controlled drinking and is successful for periods of time until he gets drunk and experiences a serious adverse consequence like the DUI he received this year. Scott has a hard time understanding his behavior. He has been able to acknowledge recently that fear of abandonment is a core problem for him. It is of such magnitude that I believe fear of abandonment is a central schema for him. He absolutely cannot be alone. On several occasions, I have given him an assignment to spend an evening home alone. He can watch television, read a book, or clean the house. He absolutely hates the experience. He maintains an excessive social life to avoid being alone. He eats out seven days a week, and

4 - SELF-EXAMINATION

despite a girlfriend who he claims to love, he is always on the lookout for another woman as a back-up.

Scott has many strengths. He is a talented craftsman and has been successful with real estate investments. He works hard and is open to new experiences. Interestingly, he likes both SMART Recovery and A.A., and has found meetings in both programs that he attends. Oddly, he does not have a problem with the different and distinct philosophies of each program. He feels both programs have their strengths and he gets something out of both. Now that he has received a DUI, his meeting attendance will be mandatory, and I have every confidence he will be actively involved.

I think Scott will struggle with sobriety as long as his deep-seated fear of abandonment and dislike of being alone continue to put him in danger zones like bars, golf club venues, and restaurant happy hours. He remains resistant to taking the medications Antabuse or naltrexone, which would help mitigate these risks. He continues to come to therapy, and as the recovery community knows, "it's progress, not perfection."

BRIAN'S SELF-EXAMINATION

Brian has worked long and hard on his recovery from drugs and alcohol. He has deep introspection and great self-awareness. He recognizes that he suffers from what we call a co-occurring disorder, meaning he has to be concerned about two things: his addiction to mood-altering chemicals and his diagnosed depression.

Brian is under the care of a psychiatrist and takes antidepressant medication regularly. He has studied to be a substance abuse counselor, so he is well-educated on the relapse potential of his situation. During *his self-examination process, he recognized that if or when he stops the self-management of one problem, i.e., addiction, he becomes vulnerable to a recurrence of his depression. Conversely, if he abruptly stops his medication and management of his depression, the "negative committee" will appear in full force and destabilize his sobriety. Simply put, we call this "taking care of both sides of the street."*

Individuals with mental health issues in addition to drug and alcohol problems need to monitor both problems to remain successful. Unfortunately, for many addicts and alcoholics over the years, the treatment community has been divided into different camps. The mental health professionals and substance abuse professionals were not cross-trained, nor did they usually work with one another. This lack of knowledge caused the loss of many souls.

Fortunately, there has been great improvement in this area over the last fifteen years. The "Collective Wisdom" is now clear, "BOTH MENTAL HEALTH AND DRUG AND ALCOHOL ISSUES MUST BE MANAGED TOGETHER FOR RECOVERY TO BE STABLE."

Brian has many strengths that have grown in recovery. He was able to handle a serious and extremely painful relationship breakup without relapse or hospitalization. It was a challenge, and I will discuss this in further detail in a subsequent chapter. However, Brian, at the end of the experience, understood how truly resilient and healthy he had become. He is now dating again. He checks in periodically and he continues to work a very active program of recovery.

4 - SELF-EXAMINATION

SAMANTHA'S SELF-EXAMINATION

As previously discussed, Samantha had worked hard on her recovery and addressed many issues both with her N.A. sponsor and in therapy. She was smart and worked hard to advance in school. She had an excellent rapport with her fellow students and was well liked. Samantha was insightful, humorous, and extremely empathic. All of these strengths fueled her progress.

There is an expression in the recovery community: "we are as sick as our secrets." Sammy's inability to work through her schema of emotional deprivation led her to continue to work secretly as a prostitute. I believe pursuing that lifestyle powered her downfall. Her insatiable need for outside attention and the financial rewards it generated were stronger than her ability to self-nurture and self-sooth. Ultimately, she returned to drugs for the soothing and comfort she so desperately needed.

Sammy's story provides us with another piece of "Collective Wisdom": "YOU CANNOT CHERRY PICK WHAT PARTS OF RECOVERY YOU WILL ENGAGE IN, AND WHICH PARTS YOU WILL NOT."

Half measures do not work. Think of a war battleground. You may have a good number of troops and resources protecting several key areas. But if you leave one area unprotected and vulnerable, that is where the enemy will likely strike. The "negative committee" is masterful at determining where you are at risk and that is where it will strike to destabilize and take you down.

ESTELLA'S SELF-EXAMINATION

As mentioned previously, Estella had a very loving and stable childhood. She grew up with self-esteem and confidence. But years of living with Carl eroded much of what she understood about herself. As a woman in her late fifties, she grew up valuing long-term marriage and family. Upon serious self-examination, she realized that she fought the guilt connected with leaving her alcoholic husband on a daily basis. This was soon coupled with severe resentment created by his poor treatment of her during the divorce proceedings. Despite her kindness and real empathy toward him, he was mean and vindictive.

In therapy, she recognized that it wasn't the possessions or actual finances that upset her as much as the message he was sending about her value and their 20-plus years together. She said she felt like she was on a seesaw. One day she was wracked with guilt over walking out on him, the next day she was enraged at his condescension and mean-spirited financial proposals. He spent huge sums of money on his attorneys in an effort to punish her.

It became clear to Estella that letting go of her resentments and managing her emotions were critical to her ability to remain clean and sober. We talked extensively about the connections between our thoughts, feelings, and actions. My friend, colleague, and frequent co-author Bill Eddy outlines this simple concept with me in our recently published client manual, New Ways for Work [3:p.19]. Flexible thinking will lead to managed emotions, which result in more moderate behaviors.

Estella used this framework to help her cope during these difficult times. She looked at her thoughts such as "How can he treat someone so poorly that has been devoted to him for over twenty years?" and reframed them to "His alcoholism is so progressed that

4 - SELF-EXAMINATION

he cannot think clearly about his life or understand the consequences of his hateful behavior."

Over time, not taking her husband's behavior so personally helped Estella move from rage to empathy. Once Estella managed her emotions, she was able to keep her behavior constructive despite his relentless hostility.

In therapy, these cognitive-behavioral techniques helped Estella work on the issues she identified in the self-examination process. It is important to remember that just identifying an issue such as resentment is not enough. We then must take steps to actively work on the issues so they do not sabotage recovery. More detailed information about these useful techniques will follow in Chapter 10.

IN SUMMARY

The fourth theme of the PDMT Model is Self-Examination [1]. Once a person achieves abstinence, this process is necessary to identify and begin working on the issues that will impact their ability to remain clean and sober. Sometimes these issues are easy to identify, like pride or resentment. Other times it is coming to terms with a mental health disorder like depression or bipolar condition. Sometimes the issues are deep-rooted and create behavior patterns or responses that jeopardize recovery like the schemas of abandonment, defectiveness/shame, or emotional deprivation.

A careful analysis of your character assets and liabilities is an intimate and personal exploration. I recommend exploring this theme with an experienced counselor, therapist, sponsor, or support person who can provide support and insight as you undertake this challenging task.

A lack of personal responsibility often negatively impacts success at this juncture, which takes us to the heart of the next theme, Taking Responsibility [1].

FURTHER INFORMATION

12-step programs have fourth-step worksheets and study guides available for those who want to work this step in earnest and with deliberation. Various helpful checklists and resources can be found on the internet, as well as through publishers of recovery materials such as Hazelden Publishing (www.hazelden.org/).

ALCOHOLICS ANONYMOUS (A.A.)

A.A. literature tells the story of how Bill W. a stockbroker from N.Y. and Dr. Bob, a prominent surgeon, met in Akron, Ohio in 1935. Bill had recently become sober working directly with other alcoholics. Dr. Bob was struggling and unable to maintain sobriety at the time of their first meeting.

According to the program, their first encounter had an immediate effect on the doctor. Apparently, Bill explained that alcoholism was a disease, "a malady of body, mind, and emotion [4]." This is something Bill had learned in New York from the noted physician Dr. William D. Silkworth. Although Dr. Bob was also a physician, he had never considered alcoholism to be a disease. He had thought it was a lack of willpower, as most people in those days did. Working with Bill W., he soon became sober and never drank again [4].

4 - SELF-EXAMINATION

Both men immediately began to work with alcoholics in Akron with this new conceptualization of alcoholism as a disease. In the fall of 1935 in New York, a second group formed and began to meet. A third was started in Cleveland in 1939. According to A.A. literature, it took over four years to obtain one hundred sober alcoholics from the three initial groups [4].

Publication of the book *Alcoholics Anonymous* followed in early 1939 [5]. In this text, Bill W. explains A.A.'s philosophy and methods, including the now well-known Twelve Steps of recovery. Dr. Bob and Bill W. also created an over-all trusteeship for the new fellowship. In what is considered by many a stroke of brilliance, they determined that non-alcoholics and recovering alcoholics would both become members of the board [5].

They opened an office in New York to assist in the growth of the fellowship. In March 1941, the *Saturday Evening Post* featured a very positive article about A.A. and the response from the public was enormous. By the end of that year, membership exceeded 6,000 and the number of A.A. groups multiplied in proportion. Further, the fellowship spread across both the United States and Canada [4].

According to A.A. historical data, by 1946 Bill W. had codified the operating principals of A.A. in what are called the Twelve Traditions of Alcoholics Anonymous [4]. This has been, by almost any standard of measurement, an amazingly successful formula for A.A. cohesion and functioning.

In 1950, A.A. held its first international convention in Cleveland, Ohio. Dr. Bob made his final public appearance at that event. His last talk focused on "keeping A.A. simple." At that convention, he witnessed the Twelve Traditions of A.A. adopted for the permanent use of the A.A. fellowship worldwide. Dr. Bob died in November of 1950, having devoted the last 15 years of his life to assisting alcoholics and the development of the A.A. program.

In 1951, the program created the A.A. General Service Conference to ensure overall functioning of the organization. In January 1971, Bill W. died of pneumonia in Miami, Florida. Earlier that year he spoke at the 35th Anniversary Convention. He had lived long enough to see the organization he nurtured grow exponentially [4].

A.A. has truly become a global fellowship. It transcends race, creed, and language barriers. A world service meeting has been held biennially since 1972 in locations around the globe. The 2020 International Convention of A.A. is scheduled to be held in July in Detroit, Michigan. The theme is "Love and Tolerance is our Code." A.A. members and guests from around the world will celebrate A.A.'s 85th year.

I had the great privilege of being an invited "honored guest" at the 2005 International Convention in Toronto, Canada to celebrate A.A.'s 70th year. Over 40,000 A.A. members and guests gathered that summer. Over 75 countries were represented at the four-day event, including, for the first time, Cuba and the People's Republic of China. The opening meeting at Roger's Centre featured an incredible flag ceremony.

Members from each participating country carried their national flag past a cheering stadium of ecstatic people. It captured so vividly the breadth and composition of the fellowship and the worldwide support it has. It was a profoundly moving experience to witness firsthand the collective joy, gratitude, love, and fellowship. It's

4 - SELF-EXAMINATION

something I will never forget. It was a deep honor to be invited and recognized by the fellowship.

Whenever I work with clients, I can say without hesitation or reservation that I have met thousands of people in A.A. who are self-described miracles of recovery. It certainly may not be the answer for every alcoholic looking for support, but it deserves serious consideration as its benefits are enormous, and its miracles real.

The Twelve Steps of A.A. [2]

1. We admitted we were powerless over alcohol - that our lives had become unmanageable.
2. Came to believe that a Power greater than ourselves could restore us to sanity.
3. Made a decision to turn our will and our lives over to the care of God as we understood Him.
4. Made a searching and fearless moral inventory of ourselves.
5. Admitted to God, to ourselves and to another human being the exact nature of our wrongs.
6. Were entirely ready to have God remove all these defects of character.
7. Humbly asked Him to remove our shortcomings.
8. Made a list of all persons we had harmed, and became willing to make amends to them all.
9. Made direct amends to such people wherever possible, except when to do so would injure them or others.
10. Continued to take personal inventory and when we were wrong promptly admitted it.

11. Sought through prayer and meditation to improve our conscious contact with God as we understood Him, praying only for knowledge of His will for us and the power to carry that out.
12. Having had a spiritual awakening as the result of these steps, we tried to carry this message to alcoholics and to practice these principles in all our affairs.

NARCOTICS ANONYMOUS (NA)

Narcotics Anonymous was founded in 1953. According to their literature, their membership growth was minimal for their first 20 years as an organization. They published a basic text in 1983 and thereafter their membership and meetings dramatically increased.

Currently, NA facilitates over 67,000 meetings weekly in 139 countries. Their program is also based on the Twelve Steps. They offer an ongoing support network for addicts who wish to maintain a drug-free life. NA makes no distinction between drugs, including alcohol [6].

ADDITIONAL SUPPORT GROUPS AND RESOURCES

COCAINE ANONYMOUS	https://ca.org/
MARIJUANA ANONYMOUS	https://www.marijuana-anonymous.org/
NICOTINE ANONYMOUS	https://nicotine-anonymous.org/
PILLS ANONYMOUS	www.pillsanonymous.org
CRYSTAL METH ANONYMOUS (CMA)	https://crystalmeth.org/
I HATE HEROIN	http://www.ihateheroin.org/

4 - SELF-EXAMINATION

Please note that many of these groups have meetings in countries around the world and literature translated into a number of languages. Also, mobile apps, helplines, and online meetings are available with some organizations, and most host periodic world conferences.

OTHER RELATED SUPPORT GROUPS

GAMBLERS ANONYMOUS (GA)	www.gamblersanonymous.org
SEXAHOLICS ANONYMOUS	https://www.sa.org/
OVEREATERS ANONYMOUS	https://oa.org/
FOR FAMILY MEMBERS (more information in Chapter 5)	
AL-ANON	www.al-anon.alateen.org
NAR-ANON	www.nar-anon.org/
LEARN 2 COPE	http://www.learn2cope.org/
S-ANON (for family members of sex addicts)	https://www.sanon.org/

RECOVERY TREATMENT AND SERVICES

Recovery.org

This website provides information in locating treatment and recovery services throughout the United States. They provide resources for 12-step and non-12-step services. They offer assistance in locating dual-diagnosis recovery programs for mental health and substance use disorders. [7]

Substance Abuse and Mental Health Services Administration: SAMHSA

This federal agency was created to improve the quality and availability of services in order to reduce problems related to substance abuse and mental illness [8]. It provides a national behavioral health treatment services locator. This is a confidential and anonymous source of information for people seeking treatment facilities and services for substance and mental health problems in the United States [9]. They also have a national helpline: 1-800-662-HELP (4357), 1-800-487-4889 (TDD)

CANADIAN RESOURCES

Canadian Centre on Substance Abuse: CCSA

The Canadian Parliament created this Centre to provide leadership in addressing substance use in Canada. It provides guidance, resources, and up-to-date research information [10].

Ontario Drug and Alcohol Helpline
Formerly: Drug and Alcohol Registry of Treatment (DART)

This Canadian resource provides free and confidential, bilingual, drug and alcohol information and referral services within Ontario. Their assistance is provided live, 24/7, by phone, email or web chat. It is a service of ConnexOntario, a health service information organization funded by the Ontario Government [11]. 1-800-565-8603.

4 - SELF-EXAMINATION

Centre for Addiction and Mental Health: CAMH

This organization is known as the "largest mental health and addiction teaching hospital" in Canada. It is also "one of the world's leading research centres in the area of addiction and mental health." CAMH is committed to providing comprehensive, accessible care for people who have problems with addiction and mental illness. "A wide range of clinical programs, support and rehabilitation services are provided that meet the diverse needs" of this population [12]. 1-800-463-2338.

Addictions Foundation Manitoba: AFM

AFM provides prevention, treatment, research and educational services for alcohol and other substance abuse. This agency provides services for adults, families, and youth at 28 locations across the province [13]. 1-800-463-1554.

REFERENCE LIST

[1] L.G. DiStefano, LCSW and M. Hohman, Ph.D., *The Paradigm Developmental Model of Treatment: A Clinical Guide for Counselors Working with Substance Abusers and the Chemically Dependent.* San Diego, CA: Montezuma Publishing, 2010.

[2] Alcoholics Anonymous World Services, Inc. (2016, Aug.). *The Twelve Steps of Alcoholics Anonymous* [Online]. Available: http://www.aa.org/assets/en_US/smf-121_en.pdf

[3] B. Eddy, LCSW, Esq. and L.G. Distefano, LCSW, *New Ways for Work: Personal Skills for Productive Relationships: Coaching Manual.* Scottsdale, AZ: High Conflict Institute Press, 2015, p. 19.

[4] Alcoholics Anonymous World Services, Inc. (2017) *Historical Data: The Birth of A.A. and its Growth in the US/Canada.* [Online]. Available: www.aa.org/pages/en_US/historical-data-the-birth-of-aa-and-its-growth-in-the-uscanada

[5] B. Smith, Dr. and B. Wilson, *Alcoholics Anonymous, The Big Book.* New York, NY: Alcoholics Anonymous World Services, Inc. 2001.

[6] Narcotics Anonymous World Services. (2017). *Information about NA* [Online]. Available: http://www.na.org/?ID=PR-index

[7] Recovery.org. (2017). *Choose the Best Addiction Recovery Program for You* [Online]. Available: www.recovery.org

[8] Substance Abuse and Mental Health Services Administration. *About Us* [Online]. Available: https://www.samhsa.gov/about-us

[9] Substance Abuse and Mental Health Services Administration. *Behavioral Health Treatment Services Locator* [Online]. Available: https://findtreatment.samhsa.gov/

[10] Canadian Centre On Substance Abuse (CCSA). (2017). *About CCSA* [Online]. Available: http://www.cclt.ca/Eng/About-CCSA/Pages/default.aspx

[11] Ontario Drug and Alcohol Helpline (DAH). (2017) *Free Health Services Information* [Online]. Available: http://www.drugandalcoholhelpline.ca/

[12] CAMH—Center for Addiction and Mental Health. (2012). *About CAMH: Who We Are* [Online]. Available: http://www.camh.ca/en/hospital/about_camh/who_we_are/Pages/who_we_are.aspx

[13] AFM - Addictions Foundation of Manitoba. *About AFM* [Online]. Available: https://afm.mb.ca/about-afm/

CHAPTER 5

THEME 5
TAKING RESPONSIBILITY

LARRY'S STORY

The family counselor received a call from Larry's wife. She was beside herself. Apparently, the couple got into a furious fight, and Larry barged out of the house threatening to get high and ruin his new sobriety. That evening Larry walked into his outpatient group session, which I was facilitating. He had a sheepish grin on his face, and when our eyes met, I realized he knew his wife had called.

When the session began, I asked Larry if he had anything he wanted to share. He launched into a tirade about how hard it was to stay off drugs when you had a wife who would nag at you for any number of insane reasons. As Larry began to wind down, I asked him to take a breath and consider the following thought. I said, "Larry, let's suppose that next week you find out something horrible like your wife has spent all the money in your mutual bank account or, perhaps worse than that, she took the money and had run off with your best friend. Would you be so angry at her that you would cut off your balls?" He looked incredulous. "You heard me! Would you get so mad at something your wife did that you would cut off your balls?"

Group members laughed hysterically and later told me that he actually closed his legs as he replied. He said, "Georgi, I would never do that." But I pushed, "Larry, would you cut your balls off for a million dollars? What about five million? Wouldn't you cut off your balls for five million?!" At this point Larry was furious. "Georgi, no damn amount of money is worth cutting off my balls!"

I sat back in my chair and looked Larry straight in the eye. "Well Larry, I suppose when your sobriety becomes as important as your balls you'll be in recovery."

5 - TAKING RESPONSIBILITY

He instantly understood and began to nod his head in agreement.

Think about it for a moment. Larry, like most men, cannot imagine anything that could be worth the horror of cutting off his genitals. Men will go to great lengths to protect this anatomy--it is not negotiable. The same analogy holds true for recovery. Men and women who are in recovery often must go to great lengths to protect their recovery. They recognize that recovery is more important than a relationship because there will be no relationship without recovery. They realize recovery is more important than a job because there will be no job (over time) without recovery. There will be no functional family, or health, or financial wellbeing without recovery. Therefore, recovery must come first.

Drinking or using can no longer be an option. You must protect recovery at all costs. I call this the "psychological primacy" of recovery. Through working with addicts and alcoholics over the years, my ears became trained to hear statements that either supported the primacy of recovery or minimized the relevance of recovery in someone's life.

For example, when you hear a client say that they didn't have time to attend any recovery activities during the week, it's generally an indication that the primacy of recovery has not taken hold. On the other hand, when you see a client reworking their schedule to accommodate aspects of their recovery program, such as family therapy or a support meeting, that's an excellent sign that recovery is a central and primary focus in that person's life.

The self-help fellowship, Secular Organization for Sobriety, emphasizes the priority of sobriety as a tenet and central guideline of their program [1].

THEME 5 - TAKING RESPONSIBILITY

This theme is central to ongoing recovery. The fact you have a disease doesn't negate the fact that only you can be truly responsible for a successful outcome. Support systems, resources, and tools can all be helpful, but ultimately the buck stops with you.

There are two components to taking responsibility. The first is the cognitive component best described above. It's the mental recognition that only if I am clean and sober can the other important elements of my life flourish. Recovery is not merely an aspect of your life. It is the unifying theme, which promotes and reaffirms your commitments to a healthy, well-balanced, and enriched life experience.

An important factor of taking responsibility is acknowledging why you haven't been successful in the past and what you will do differently this time. Perhaps you minimized the daily effort that was required. For a number of years, I had a banner in my group room that had the following equation in large letters:

$$E > DU \text{ to } = R;$$

Effort must be greater than your drug usage to equal recovery.

It's a simple formula. If you're shooting up heroin daily, going to one Narcotics Anonymous meeting per week will definitely not be sufficient. If you're drinking a bottle of wine nightly, with no real plan or way to objectively measure cutting back, the cutting back will probably not last.

5 - TAKING RESPONSIBILITY

The formula demonstrates the second component of taking responsibility. The E stands for effort, which predominantly is behavioral. You can't think your way to sustained sobriety, you must behave your way into recovery. Remember the Smart Doctor discussed in Chapter 2. He was a brilliant man who could not accept that he couldn't think his way out of his disease.

Behavior counts in recovery. In treatment, behavior is such an important factor that the therapy is not just referred to as cognitive, but cognitive-behavioral. Years ago, when I ran treatment groups five days a week, I realized that I tried to listen for the clients who were beginning to move into behaviors within the first two weeks of program participation. They might say, "I called someone who gave me their number at a meeting," or "I've been reading about relapse prevention." Calling and reading are both actions.

On a deeper level, after a person has completed a thorough self-examination, they would have identified problems and issues that could prevent their success. Part of taking responsibility is to address those issues. "What changes in behavior and attitude can improve the situation? Do I need to increase my tolerance for imperfection? How will I go about that? Do I need to become more empathic toward others? What can I regularly do to increase my empathic responses? Do I need to remove my ego from my decision-making? Do I need to be more rigorously honest in my dealings with others? How do I accomplish that? Do my resentments create a cycle that triggers cravings? What is my plan to address my resentments and deal with them?"

As clients identify and address these types of issues, the process of taking responsibility begins to occur. Taking responsibility is a healthy response after careful self-examination.

Another important aspect is to identify your strengths. Why? Strengths reinforce our resiliencies and confidence. Let's say that you communicate very well and are articulate. That strength can serve you well in recovery. This means you could decide to push yourself and speak more frequently in support meetings. By speaking more frequently you improve your communication skills, which helps you to crystalize the thoughts and emotions you want to express. This process enhances your recovery. The practice of speaking more frequently also benefits your performance at work, helping to improve your self-esteem and relationships with colleagues.

It may take several attempts at recovery before you take full responsibility. You will know when you have. Remember my client Larry: recovery is not negotiable.

BOBBY'S STORY

Several years ago, I received a phone call from a gentleman I had treated for alcoholism 18 years previous. He was doing very well in his recovery, despite having a few brief relapses in the early years. He stated that it took him awhile to believe that he couldn't go back to occasional use without adverse consequences. The near loss of his marriage and renewal of his spiritual life helped to recommit his efforts, and he now had over a decade of sobriety. It is always gratifying to learn that your clients are successful, however in this case Joe still needed my assistance, but it was for his son Bobby. He asked to bring Bobby in for an assessment.

Bobby was 19 years old and in the eyes of the law, a legal adult. I had to make it clear that I could not

5 - TAKING RESPONSIBILITY

talk about Bobby without his permission, and to keep boundaries clear I would not discuss him without his presence. Bobby was involved with a number of serious drugs including Oxycontin (a narcotic pain reliever) and black tar heroin, which he snorted. He also drank excessively and smoked marijuana.

Bobby was vulnerable and somewhat open for help. I arranged for immediate inpatient treatment at a local facility, which he accepted, followed by several months in a residential program and sober living environment. Although my office was a considerable distance away, we arranged for him to see me in weekly individual therapy. We added family therapy once he completed his initial treatment program.

Bobby had a good number of strengths and support. He had a loving, intact family that understood addiction. He had an older brother that provided a good deal of encouragement and companionship. Bobby was bright and had graduated high school but was floundering in community college due to his drug usage. He dropped out of school to focus on his rehabilitation activities.

The great challenge for Bobby was to create a support system outside his family and take responsibility for his recovery. We had many sessions focused on the fact that he knew he could deceive his family at least temporarily and continue using. He could do the same with me. It was not an easy undertaking for Bobby, and I have met many older more mature individuals who could not accomplish what he set out to do.

The residential program helped him deal with urges and cravings in a safe environment. He asked his parents to return home after a short time in the sober living environment, and I supported his request. Their relationship was healthy, and they helped to mitigate the loneliness he constantly experienced. Bobby's brother was an invaluable resource. Only four years older, he involved Bobby in activities that were "cool" but did not involve drugs or alcohol like surfing and hiking.

To remain clean and sober, Bobby had to give up "people, places, and things." He even took his father to his drug dealer. Joe told the dealer that if he sold Bobby drugs again that he would notify the police. It was a risky move, but Joe's physically imposing stature and assertiveness proved effective. Bobby knew he could always find drugs, but it was not going to be from that individual. Bobby relapsed briefly on a few occasions but appeared to learn from each episode. He also relapsed on pot and alcohol but not opioids, which made reengagement in his program easier as it did not require medical management.

Call it great luck or divine intervention, but a major component of success for Bobby occurred almost by accident. He had wanted to ride a motorcycle for years. His parents staunchly opposed the idea given his mother's nursing background. She had seen far too many head traumas in her career to sanction purchasing a motorcycle. I felt equally as concerned but became Bobby's strongest advocate in family therapy for the approval of the motorcycle. Why? Bobby had met an older man at an A.A. meeting who had a motorcycle and who went on weekly weekend rides to the mountains with a group of recovering alcoholic/addicts. Although they were older than Bobby, the shared interest in motorcycles and sobriety, along with weekly trips to the local mountains or along the coast was a strong incentive. Bobby desperately needed a tonic for the loneliness and

5 - TAKING RESPONSIBILITY

alienation he felt since separating from his peers who continued to drink and use.

Bobby proved an effective negotiator. He could purchase the bike and store it at his parents' home under the condition that he complete two motorcycle safety courses. Bobby threw himself into the task and completed the requirement in record time. His timing was also perfect. He bought a great motorcycle with the help of his A.A. friend. It was the beginning of spring, and he enjoyed weekly rides with his new friends. It was clear he was learning a tremendous amount of collective wisdom from these recovering individuals who were members of both N.A. and A.A.

We spent many sessions discussing what he learned, and to tell the truth, it was much more impactful and relevant to him than months of formal treatment. That is not to say that the formal treatment was not a necessary foundation, but I am convinced that his relationships with the bikers proved to be an absolutely essential ingredient in his recovery journey.

Another factor proved significant: Bobby did not want to return to college. He did not know what he wanted to pursue and felt little motivation to attend. Also, he feared the alcohol/drug scene that existed on campus and didn't want to be hyper vigilant on a daily basis in such an environment. What he did want was a job, and when an excellent opportunity arose at the company for which his father worked, he applied for it. He understood that the company did random drug testing and he seemed to appreciate the additional accountability.

Bobby was lucky. His father's connections ensured him an interview and he apparently impressed. It took several weeks for everything to come together and the idle time over the summer drove Bobby crazy. But he stayed clean and sober and the day finally arrived when work began. He loved the experience and adapted quickly. The job provided on-site training, which taught him a skill set that was much more meaningful than random classes at college. The job provided focus, structure, and accountability. It also fostered relationships and opportunities for growth and self-esteem.

After several months on the job, Bobby stated that he was ready to end therapy, and I concurred. We agreed that he should locate a therapist closer to his home/job if he wanted to resume therapy as issues came up. At the time he completed treatment, he was clean/sober and was actively involved in 12-step meetings. He had a close group of recovering bikers that he saw on the weekends and a supportive family well educated about the disease and recovery process. He had a job that he had become comfortable with and enjoyed.

Despite all these positives, remaining clean/sober at such a young age is a major challenge. He recently achieved four years of continuous clean/sober time. He never felt the need to go back to therapy but did change his N.A. sponsor and has worked steps again.

I would point out three key factors that promoted Bobby's success, in addition to a supportive family. Bobby took responsibility for his recovery in both his thoughts and actions. He traveled a long distance to see me once to twice per week. He attended meetings and worked the traditional Twelve Steps with a sponsor and the PDMT cognitive themes with me in therapy. He changed the proverbial "people, places, and things" to reduce cravings and temptations. He found a group of friends in recovery with a common set of interests and focused on activities that supported his sobriety. Finally, he found work that was meaningful and required accountability. Bobby's success at such a young age defies the odds and proves again that recovery is achievable.

In the book *Treating Addiction: A Guide for Professionals*, William Miller and his co- authors state, "Employment is a strong predictor of sobriety." They double down on this assertion by stating, "Discharging a client to unemployment is an invitation to failure [2:p.187]." Helping and motivating clients to find meaningful work does much to enhance their post-treatment sobriety and should be an important consideration.

In addition, the client's social support network is a very strong predictor of ongoing recovery. According to the authors, "Those who have a strong social network in support of sobriety are significantly more likely to achieve it [2:p.188]." In Bobby's case, the bikers' group played a significant role in supporting Bobby's recovery, as did his engagement in a meaningful job.

RON'S STORY

Ron contacted me several years ago. A friendly and intelligent graphic designer for a large private company, he was afraid of losing his job and his marriage. A friend suggested he speak with me, and it was clear that he had suffered tremendously from his drinking problem. He identified as alcoholic and had attempted sobriety on numerous occasions only to fall back to drinking. While he had used other drugs in college, now in his thirties he preferred alcohol.

After a careful assessment, it was evident that he also suffered from a mental health problem: bipolar disorder. This is a mental disorder marked by alternating periods of elation and depression [3]. There are several types of bipolar and related disorders, and symptoms can vary from person to person. In Ron's case, he suffered from Bipolar II. He experienced unpredictable changes in mood and behavior, as well as depressive episodes and less frequently, hypomanic episodes. Some of his symptoms included inflated self-esteem (which created many job difficulties), unusual talkativeness, racing thoughts, and distractibility. He would also experience depressed mood, reduced interest or pleasure in activities, loss of energy, and feelings of worthlessness. This was all on top of the symptoms associated with hangovers and alcohol cravings.

After we managed Ron's alcohol detox and a psychiatrist stabilized his bipolar condition with medication, we began therapy in earnest. Ron recognized that his wife, Therese, was at the end of her rope, so he agreed to take Antabuse to increase his ability to stay sober and calm the marital waters.

Ron knew he had a serious alcohol problem and identified as an alcoholic. He also knew he had mental health issues. However, he never linked the two conditions or recognized their interrelationship. Our initial work centered on problem recognition for both conditions. Ron learned that if he did not attend to the signs and symptoms of his bipolar condition, they would escalate and trigger urges and cravings to self-medicate with alcohol. Conversely, if Ron began to escalate his drinking, he would create the environment for depression and irritability to take hold. Understanding these dynamics was essential for Ron to be able to succeed in early recovery.

Ron worked hard on his recovery. He attended several SMART Recovery meetings but surprisingly found A.A. more relevant to him despite his reservations with the spiritual aspects. He settled on two meetings each week plus a structured step study. He remained in weekly individual therapy for two years, followed by alternating individual and couples therapy. He has not engaged with a sponsor, which was not unanticipated given his fear of authoritarian control. His father was a bully and very demeaning. Ron is aware of the connection between his father and his hesitancy to engage with a sponsor and continues to work on that issue. He has had two short relapses (two to three days) over the last 36 months, each time he had stopped taking his Antabuse prior to drinking. He has been able to take responsibility for his self-sabotage. Today his job is stable and his marriage is doing very well. Moreover, Ron is giving back to the recovery community. He is involved in homelessness projects and bringing recovery literature and materials to the local hospitals. Ron recognizes that his co-occurring disorder places him at high risk to relapse and that he must take responsibility and address both of his conditions regularly. He demonstrates this commitment on a daily basis.

CO-OCCURRING DISORDERS

I would like to take a moment and reflect on the historical aspects of what we call co-occurring disorders. When I began working in this field as a social worker in the late 1970s and early 1980s, very few agencies or treatment programs worked with both addiction and mental health problems. Their services existed in silos; most alcohol/drug treatment did not address mental health issues, and most mental health programs did not address alcohol and drug problems.

This was terribly unfortunate, and literally thousands of individuals across the country needlessly relapsed and suffered from the treatment community's lack of knowledge and expertise in this area. Professionals only addressed the most blatant of cases, which usually meant that AOD treatment stopped until they could stabilize the mental health condition. However, it took many more years for the treatment community to understand the interrelationship between AOD issues and mental health diagnosis. Today we understand that individuals must have strong treatment plans that address "both sides of the street" if individuals are to maintain their recovery.

It should be noted that an individual may need to remain abstinent for several months before a professional can make a reliable mental health diagnosis. Nevertheless, the sooner you engage a mental health provider for assistance, the better.

YOUNG ADULTS AND CO-OCCURRING DISORDERS

Despite advances in the coordination and integration of services for both addiction and mental health treatment, an area in desperate need of attention involves young adults. Once a child turns 18, parents become considerably restricted in their ability to interface with the treatment community.

Obviously at some point, an individual becomes an adult and takes responsibility for themselves. Strict confidentiality and privacy restrictions bind our medical community. These are appropriate and important measures. However, for the young adult who suffers from paranoia or psychosis, this can create considerable difficulty. A psychosis is "A severe medical condition in which thoughts and emotions are so impaired that contact is frequently lost with external reality [4]." Paranoia is "A mental condition characterized by delusions of persecution... [5]." There is suspicion and mistrust of people or their actions without evidence or justification [5].

Add the consumption of alcohol, marijuana, and/or other substances to a situation where a mental health disorder is suspected, and it becomes apparent how difficult navigating treatment options for a resistive young adult can be.

RODRIGO'S FAMILY'S STORY

Several years ago, Martina, a mother of an 18-year-old, came into therapy for her own support and stress management. She was struggling with trying to determine appropriate boundaries with her son. She had learned about co-dependency and was attempting to respond in effective and healthy ways, but was becoming increasingly concerned about her son's mental health. He had left home shortly after high school graduation to pursue work in Phoenix, Arizona. Despite a booming job market at the time, he managed to lose three different jobs. During their telephone conversations, he complained about not thinking clearly and that people were staring at him. He became worried about the "electrical fields" around his rented room.

Martina knew that her son smoked pot and urged him to quit, initially believing that it was the cause of the symptoms he was experiencing. Over the course of three years, the symptoms increased, as did her son's refusal to engage in on-going treatment. Martina was able to convince him to see a psychiatrist for one appointment. The doctor stated that Rodrigo was clinically depressed and may have other disorders, but his use of marijuana and other possible substances compromised a diagnosis.

Several other attempts at motivating Rodrigo into treatment failed. He would go for an assessment or several sessions of outpatient treatment only to quit. His family had great difficulty obtaining information or coordinating care. His behavior became increasingly erratic. He was quiet and vulnerable one minute and aggressive and demanding the next. He became violent. Eventually, he was hospitalized requiring both forced restraint and forced medication. He was diagnosed with schizoaffective disorder and assigned a caseworker.

Despite the diligence of the family and the sincere efforts of the caseworker, the system itself created great obstacles. There were legal issues that Rodrigo created due to his illness. According to Martina, there were times that he was able to reason and act in his own interest. However, he apparently could not sustain that behavior. He refused medication and continues to use marijuana intermittently. One of the most frustrating problems was that he had to sign documents to receive social security disability assistance and adamantly refused. Although he slept on a couch in Martina's small home and had no money, and Martina had limited resources, he was afraid of the government and refused assistance. This story has many disappointing components related to the failure of our social service, legal, and medical systems. Martina has recognized that it will continue to be a long, difficult challenge. She is committed to helping her son, as is her boyfriend.

5 - TAKING RESPONSIBILITY

Nevertheless, our current system makes it very difficult for parents of adult children to be actively involved in the coordination of services and interventions frequently needed by young adults who suffer from both substance abuse and mental health disorders. Currently, an individual must experience a number of short-term hospitalizations with increasing deterioration before longer-term involuntary treatment options become authorized and available.

Unless young adults are willing to take medication, which they frequently are not, they continue to deteriorate. They become stuck in a cycle of increasing deterioration that poses considerable risk to their wellbeing. On the streets of our cities, one needs only to see the mentally ill homeless to understand how destitute, vulnerable, and compromised an individual can become. The homeless is also a group with a large subgroup composed of many individuals with substance abuse and mental illness.

We need significant resources and committed action on both the state and national level to design and implement effective treatment services for these vulnerable populations. Many of these individuals sadly end up involved in the criminal justice system because of their cognitive difficulties and frequent erratic behavior, rather than the mental health system.

I want to acknowledge the gallant efforts of social workers, nurses, doctors, counselors, police emergency response teams and other professionals and volunteers who work diligently to deliver services to our mental health communities. We need to listen to treatment providers and family members in order to create viable solutions to these complicated issues. Those individuals working on the front lines offer an abundance of relevant and important insights.

FURTHER INFORMATION

FAMILY AND MENTAL HEALTH RESOURCES

Al-Anon Family Groups

This is a free support group with meetings across the country for friends and families of problem drinkers. In Al-Anon/Alateen, members do not give advice to one another. Instead, they share their own personal experiences and stories. Often times, individuals will seek professional counseling and utilize Al-Anon for additional ongoing support [6].

Co-Dependents Anonymous: CoDA

This is a support group for recovery from codependence. This group addresses the patterns and characteristics of codependence. Members learn to identify denial, compliance, low self-esteem, avoidance, and control patterns. Some members were raised in families with substance abuse problems and/or other dysfunctional behavior that led to the development of these characteristics and patterns. This program can also be used as an adjunct to professional therapy or as an on-going support system [7].

National Alliance On Mental Illness: NAMI

This organization, with hundreds of volunteers across the country, provides help and hope to millions of Americans suffering from mental illness. According to their literature, they fight stigma, raise awareness, provide support, and educate the public. They provide mental health advocacy and strive to improve public policy [8]. They have established 2017 National Policy

Priorities and are working diligently to safeguard mental health benefits [9].

Dual Recovery Anonymous: DRA

DRA "...is an independent, non-professional, Twelve Step, self-help membership organization for people with a dual diagnosis. Our goal is to help men and women who experience a dual illness. We are chemically dependent and we are also affected by an emotional or psychiatric illness. Both illnesses affect us in all areas of our lives; physically, psychologically, socially, and spiritually [10]." This program provides a much-needed resource in our communities. Their website is created and maintained by Dual Recovery Anonymous World Network Inc. The website provides a wealth of helpful information.

Beyond Addiction: How Science and Kindness Help People Change

This innovative and state of the art book is a must read for families. Based on the well-researched and highly regarded CRAFT program (Community Reinforcement and Family Training) for families. This text offers an abundance of important, useful, and effective information. The methods outlined in this book can contribute significantly to successful outcomes [11].

REFERENCE LIST

[1]   Secular Organizations for Sobriety (SOS). 2016. *Homepage* [Online]. Available: www.sossobriety.org

[2]   W.R. Miller, et al., *Treating Addiction: A Guide for Professionals*. New York, NY: Guilford Press, 2011, pp. 187, 188.

[3]   American Psychiatric Association, *Diagnostic and Statistical Manual of Mental Disorders*, 5th ed. Arlington, VA: American Psychiatric Association Publishing, 2013

[4]   Oxford University Press: English Oxford Living Dictionaries. (2017). *psychosis* [Online]. Available: https://en.oxforddictionaries.com/definition/us/psychosis

[5]   Oxford University Press: English Oxford Living Dictionaries. (2017). *paranoia* [Online]. Available: https://en.oxforddictionaries.com/definition/us/paranoia

[6]   Al-Anon Family Groups. (2017) *How Al-Anon/Alateen Works for Me* [Online]. Available: http://al-anon.org/how-al-anon-works-for-me

[7]   Co-Dependents Anonymous International. (2017). *Welcome to Codependents Anonymous* [Online]. Available: http://coda.org

[8]   NAMI: National Alliance on Mental Illness. (2017). *About NAMI* [Online]. Available: https://www.nami.org/About-NAMI

[9]   NAMI: National Alliance on Mental Illness. (2017). *2017 National Policy Priorities* [Online]. Available: https://www.nami.org/Learn-More/Mental-Health-Public-Policy/2017-National-Policy-Priorities

[10] Dual Recovery Anonymous. (2009). *Welcome to the DRA Online Resource Center* [Online]. Available: www.draonline.org/

[11] J. Foote, Ph.D., et al., *Beyond Addiction: How Science and Kindness Help People Change*. N.Y., New York 2014.

CHAPTER 6

THEME 6
WILLINGNESS TO CHANGE: PREPARATION TO CHANGE

JANET'S STORY

Janet raised her hand as group members took their seats. "I would like to start," she said, pulling something from her purse. She held up a plastic medicine container.

"What is that?" I asked.

"Antabuse," she responded. I was incredulous. Janet, a flight attendant, had been absolutely against using the medication as a tool. She served alcohol on flights and was afraid of skin reactions if some spilled on her. We had proposed using the tool because she was often in foreign cities, away from home, with difficulty accessing meetings that would be convenient or familiar. In addition, the negative committee is frequently more active when you are vulnerable. Being away from her support system for long periods of time made her an easy mark for the negative self-talk to convince her that one drink wouldn't hurt; who would find out?

She was adamant in her refusal and our argument fell on deaf ears, so I had instructed our program staff to leave the issue alone. Janet was cooperative in many other areas and we needed to work with that motivation. Needless to say, I was stunned when I saw the medication in her hands.

"What is this all about?" I asked.

"I was on a long flight to Paris serving our guest passengers in first class," she replied. "I have never had an urge or craving while working and always felt very comfortable serving alcohol. But on this flight a guest in first class asked me to make him a screwdriver. This is just orange juice and vodka. Well, I can't drink orange juice as I find it much too acidic, so I have never been tempted to have one.

6 - WILLINGNESS TO CHANGE

"I mixed the drink and am about to hand it over when I have a very powerful urge to drink it myself. My hands actually shook and I began to perspire. I quickly handed him the drink and went to the bathroom. I had to put cold water on my face and settle myself down. I had to return to serving but felt shaky for the rest of the flight. I couldn't tell my colleagues what was happening, so I just said my stomach was bothering me. When I returned home I went to see my doctor and got the prescription. I really thought I was in control and work was a safe place, but I can now see what people have been talking about. Just because you haven't experienced something yet doesn't mean you won't. It was foolish not to have this extra tool working for me. I have to admit; you guys were right!"

This story demonstrates Janet's willingness to change. She was fortunate that she was able to withstand the urge and not do something that would have resulted in being fired from her job. Additionally, she took steps to increase her support and defenses.

It should be noted that a trigger is usually a stimulus (person, place, issue, or thing) that will set off an impulse or compulsion to use again. Many individuals have been able to anticipate a particular trigger in advance. Their recovery plans include addressing that trigger. Other individuals have not been able to successfully anticipate triggers in advance. Those individuals can benefit in early recovery from a broad level of protection. Medications such as Antabuse or naltrexone can offer that type of assistance.

In recovery, willingness to change is a PDMT [1] cognitive theme that is a secular and cognitive interpretation of Step Six of A.A. [2]. The issue of willingness occurs throughout recovery. First, there is the willingness to abstain from alcohol/drugs. Second is the willingness to vigorously self-exam your flaws/liabilities, patterns of self-sabotage, motivations, resiliencies, and strengths. Third is the willingness to change behavior and emotional responses to support sobriety. Recovery literature helps individuals focus on necessary changes with "people, places, and things."

This can be a very difficult undertaking. The term "dry drunk" is a derogatory name for people whose emotional responses, behaviors, and attitudes are the same as when they were actively abusing substances.

A person, therefore, has to address components or elements of their life that require a potential change. As someone grows in recovery, they might see the wisdom in changing their communication style, parenting approach, or financial behavior. They also may need to address other destructive behaviors like smoking, overeating, or gambling. It is clear that recovery requires more than the cessation of alcohol and drug use. To create a sense of wellbeing, inner peace, and emotional stability, people interested in recovery must examine relevant issues and modify behaviors. To strengthen behavioral changes, the thoughts in which they are anchored must also be reinforced. This is why therapy can be helpful to individuals wanting to feel a sense of guidance and safety as they engage in change.

STAGES OF CHANGE

Successful change usually is preceded by a stage of preparation. As a matter of fact, James Prochaska and Carlo DiClemente of the University of Rhode Island developed a well-regarded stage of change model in the

1980s. It's called the Transtheoretical Model, because it is an integrative model of behavior change, that features a "Stages of Change" component. This model has been extensively written about in a number of publications and adapted for use in many settings. The Stages of Change provides a framework that describes a series of 5 stages people go through to change lifestyle habits. The model has been the basis for developing effective behavioral interventions [3].

The 5 Stages of Change are as follows:

Precontemplation:
People in this stage have no interest or desire in making a change and usually do not recognize a problem exists. They are usually "uninformed or under-informed about the consequences of their behavior [3]."

Contemplation:
At this stage, individuals begin to think about the cost of a behavior. A person is weighing the costs and benefits and contemplating whether it's something they really want to do. People can remain at this stage for a very long time because of the ambivalence involved in the decision. However, people usually intend to change in the next six months. The delay in implementing a decision is often referred to as "behavioral procrastination" [3].

Preparation:
At this stage, decision to change has been made and practical efforts occur to support this decision. People intend to take action in the immediate future, usually within 30 days. Individuals develop a plan of action in this stage and engage resources for assistance [3].

Action:
It is at this stage that behavioral change takes over and the individual initiates the actions necessary to make the change happen. This is also the stage where relapse prevention activities occur [3].

Maintenance:
This is an ongoing stage of relapse prevention and monitoring. Committed individuals have been engaged in the recovery based behavior for at least 6 months [3].

It should be noted that the highly-regarded SMART Recovery Program utilizes this change model.

PREP FOR SUCCESS

Let's return to the concept of preparation, which we associate with willingness to change. We are all familiar with vows to lose weight. How many people sign up for a gym membership after the holidays? How many people buy workout clothing or nutritional supplements etc., all to prepare to lose weight? Some people follow through, and the preparation stage helps to launch a successful change experience.

Preparation is a very important ingredient for success with alcohol and drug addictions. It's important to respect the challenges and fears associated with the preparation stage.

In my book, *The Paradigm Developmental Model of Treatment, Group Topics* [4], I discuss three emotional zones. We have our Comfort Zone, which is familiar to us; it represents what we know and our daily habits and routines. If we want to move into a Growth Zone, which would contain new and exciting challenges like recovery, we first must move through the Unknown

6 - WILLINGNESS TO CHANGE

Zone: there is no way around it. The Unknown Zone is terrifying to so many of us, including people in recovery. It's a new emotional space that has no familiarity, no clear-cut markers, or anything that helps a person feel grounded and safe. For a person to be successful in recovery, they will need to initiate new actions (rituals and routines) that anchor their recovery. To do that they will have to successfully navigate the Unknown Zone and tolerate the high degree of emotional discomfort and challenges which that zone represents. Preparation can be a valuable tool in negotiating the Unknown Zone and creating a greater likelihood for successful passage through it.

Let me give an example of a client who intermittently struggled with anxiety and was committed not to use marijuana, alcohol, or pills to deal with it. His deceased grandfather was an alcoholic, and he understood the genetic risks involved for himself. He chose to avoid prescription medication although his medical doctor did offer him options should he need them.

DANIEL'S STORY

This client Daniel, a very smart young man, was accepted to an Ivy League law school. In order to attend, he had to move from the West Coast to the East Coast. Daniel has amazing problem-solving skills, but was nevertheless anxious about the move and his ability to start the school year strong. At the beginning of summer, we discussed this issue on several therapy occasions. I taught him about the three emotional zones, and he quickly saw the relevance to his situation.

He had just spent four years at a prestigious West Coast university where he was very familiar with faculty and the ins/outs of his program requirements. He knew where to find anything on campus and how to network with his classmates. The school was his Comfort Zone. Additionally, his family and long-time friends lived only an hour away. His Comfort Zone was integrated, familiar, and supportive.

The move to the East Coast was a major change. Daniel was out of his Comfort Zone and fully into the Unknown Zone. The issue became how quickly he could turn the Unknown Zone into the much more pleasant Growth Zone and reduce his levels of anxiety.

We focused on several key areas. He decided to live off campus and was successful in soliciting two West Coast friends, who were also moving to Boston, to rent a house with him. Utilizing internet pictures, a realtor, and Skype conversations, he was able to secure an ideal place five minutes from campus. The next step was to change his plan about working as long as possible in California and leave earlier for Boston. While that resulted in a loss of income and protests of "don't go yet" from his family, the additional three weeks he gained gave him the opportunity to move into his new place, secure furniture, and become familiar with his surroundings. At my suggestion, he even made several trips to campus to become familiar with the layout and the buildings where his classes would be held. He found a local gym to join and supermarket to shop. He even discovered an online delivery service that did most of his shopping for him. By the time his law school classes began five weeks later, he was ready. He was rested and comfortable in his new house with a private bedroom. He had a great semester and loved the experience.

Now chances are this young man would have succeeded regardless, but focusing on moving through the Unknown Zone with acts of preparation contributed to his confidence and enjoyment of the experience. He would have had more money in the bank had he kept to his original plan, but making these preparation adjustments helped him create a Growth Zone in record time. His levels of anxiety remained very normal and manageable. Daniel was able to begin classes focused and prepared.

PREPARATION FOR ABSTINENCE

Over the years, clients have shared collective wisdom and other strategies that have helped them successfully prepare for the beginning of abstinence and the embrace of recovery activities. Here are a few of their suggestions:

1. Share your intention to be clean/sober with people you know in your heart love you. Stating your intentions fosters the movement from thoughts into action. It makes it real and helps us to be accountable.

2. Make your home a safe, alcohol/drug-free environment. If you live with a spouse or partner, ask them to support you in this effort. You can always go to a store for a bottle or go out and buy some drugs, but creating distance between your cravings/urges and the supply is essential for early success.

3. Get medical support. You may need to detox in a hospital or have the support of an outpatient treatment program. Understand your options and what services might be available to assist

you. Don't assume it's safe to stop using abruptly. Seek medical guidance and follow the recommendations.

4. Get honest. Become honest with yourself in all areas of your life. This will not only enhance your recovery, but it will help close the door on the "negative committee" and prevent the creation of guilt and regret that frequently leads back to using.

5. Reach out for help, and know you don't have to do this alone. There are counseling and treatment programs, fellowships, and meetings. Ask for guidance and create a support system. Don't forget the many resources that are now online.

6. Educate yourself. If you have a substance use disorder, it will not go away on its own. It's very important to understand how to manage your situation successfully. You often hear in recovery circles that "it's progress, not perfection." Your recovery does not have to be perfect. It will take time to learn how to handle any number of situations. I am fond of reminding my clients to "look for the lesson." Every situation provides a unique opportunity to learn and educate ourselves. Just make a sincere effort to keep an open mind and learn all you can from the collective wisdom of the community.

Here's a simple guide to follow as you manage your recovery. When in doubt (and you no longer have a counselor or therapist) ask a recovering person who meets the following criteria:

6 - WILLINGNESS TO CHANGE

- They have at least two years of continuous recovery.
- They actively attend a program for support (SMART Recovery, A.A., SOS, etc.).
- They are willing to share their journey and experiences.

If an issue comes up, ask for guidance and follow it. Over time you may come to value his or her input, and this person might be an excellent choice for a new friend or an A.A./NA sponsor should you become involved in that fellowship. Please note an A.A./NA Sponsor is a recovering alcoholic/addict who has worked the twelve steps of A.A./NA and agrees to assist you through understanding and implementing the twelve steps in your life.

EXAMPLES OF WILLINGNESS/PREPARATION

As we conclude this chapter, let's review some of the clients I have already discussed and note the willingness and preparation that preceded their actions to change.

Ray: Two factors stand out and demonstrate Ray's willingness and preparation: his decision to come to weekly therapy and his willingness to take the medication Antabuse.

Claude: His willingness to engage regularly in another support group, SMART Recovery, after he rejected A.A. (God issues).

Deborah: Her willingness to change medical specialties after years of medical school despite successful completion of diversion requirements.

Brian: His decision to give up his apartment and willingness to live in a sober living facility--along with his cat!

Estella: Her willingness to leave her marriage and to pursue her recovery.

Bobby: His decision to delay returning to a college campus and willingness to obtain a job in an "accountable environment."

Janet: Her willingness to take the medication Antabuse.

Ron: His willingness to actively monitor his mental health disorder (bipolar) with the same attention as he monitors his sobriety.

Daniel: His willingness to change a plan to allow more time to adapt to a new environment.

These examples help to demonstrate the changes in thinking that precede actions to change. In each situation above, the individual had to willingly enter an "Unknown Zone" and embrace a change that was either scary, difficult, unfamiliar, stressful, or challenging. To each of their credits, these decisions set the stage for a successful life or recovery experience.

FURTHER INFORMATION

SMART RECOVERY: SELF-MANAGEMENT AND RECOVERY TRAINING

- "Purpose: To help individuals gain independence from addictive behavior and lead meaningful and satisfying lives. To support the availability of choices in recovery [5]."

- "Mission: To offer no-fee, self-empowering, science-based, face-to-face and online support groups for abstaining from any substance or activity addiction [5]."

- "Vision: Think SMART Worldwide [5]!"

The SMART Recovery (SR) website states, "Our participants learn tools for addiction recovery based on the latest scientific research and participate in a worldwide community which includes free, self-empowering, science-based mutual help groups [6]."

"SMART Recovery uses evidenced-based cognitive behavioral and non-confrontational motivational enhancement techniques. Our meetings focus on the application of these techniques... [5]"

SMART Recovery has a four-point system, which helps people recover from a variety of addictions and addictive behaviors. The SMART Recovery "4-Point Program offers tools and techniques for each of the program points [7]."

SMART Recovery 4-Point Program includes [7]:
Point 1: Building and Maintaining Motivation
Point 2: Coping with Urges
Point 3: Managing Thoughts, Feelings, and Behaviors
Point 4: Living a Balanced Life

SMART Recovery meetings are educational, supportive, and include open discussion. According to their official website, they support "the scientifically informed use of psychological treatments and legally prescribed psychiatric and addiction medication [5]."

SMART Recovery is a recognized resource for substance abuse and addiction recovery by the following organizations [6]:

- American Academy of Family Physicians
- The National Institute on Drug Abuse (NIDA)

- U.S. Department of Health and Human Service
- American Society of Addiction Medicine

SMART Recovery literature makes two important points:
- "SMART Recovery tools can help you regardless of whether or not you believe addiction is a disease [5]."
- "We believe that the power to change addictive behaviors resides within each individual and does not depend upon adherence to any spiritual viewpoint. The use of religious or spiritual beliefs and practices in recovery is a personal choice and not a part of our program [5]."

SMART Recovery has had phenomenal growth. It began in 1994 after splitting with Rational Recovery [8]. It is now on six continents [9]. In 2016, SMART reported over 2,000 regular worldwide meetings [10]. Its handbook is currently in its third edition. This handbook has been translated into numerous languages including Arabic, Swedish, German, Spanish, Portuguese, and Mandarin Chinese [11]. The program is operated almost entirely by volunteers, including the Board of Directors and meeting facilitators. It is noteworthy that facilitators may be qualified individuals who are not in recovery [5]. Dr. Thomas Horvath of San Diego is the long-time President of SMART Recovery.

AN APOLOGY

Not only should clients grow in their recovery and be willing to change as needed, but as therapists and counselors, so should we. It Is a tremendous responsibility to assist an individual grappling with their substance abuse issues. We need to remain informed, keep up with research and treatment advances, community resources, and medication options. We also need to adjust our thinking as new evidence becomes available.

I need to offer Dr. Thomas Horvath and SMART Recovery an apology. Back in the mid-1990s when SR was in its infancy, Dr. Horvath came to my clinic in San Diego, Counseling and Recovery Institute (CRI), to tell me about this new program. Our discussion took place over 20 years ago, and I cannot recall the specifics of the conversation. Nevertheless, I clearly remember being less than gracious to Dr. Horvath. I was skeptical about referring clients to a program that had no research at that point and few endorsements. I was also concerned that while Dr. Horvath enjoyed a stellar reputation, other clinicians could use the program as a way to market their private practices. I was keenly aware of all the possible downside consequences.

Unfortunately, I did not appreciate the remarkable contribution Dr. Horvath and his colleagues were attempting to make. He and his colleagues recognized very early that individuals needed a variety of options for recovery and that one program (A.A.) did not meet the needs of everyone. There are individuals who do not want a spiritually-based program, nor a sponsor or set of steps to follow. Many individuals enjoy the cross-talk and discussions that SR facilitates. Some individuals do not feel their addiction is a disease. SR embraces those individuals too. So in hindsight, it is clear what a tremendous contribution this program has made. Today it is the largest of the non-12-step mutual self-help groups.

However, back in the mid-1990s I was skeptical and not at all encouraging.

I was wrong. SMART Recovery has earned its excellent reputation and deserves to be supported as a legitimate and important recovery resource. Dr. Horvath and his colleagues also deserve our gratitude and admiration for persevering through what must have been many challenging days and issues to bring us this beautifully crafted program.

BOOK RECOMMENDATION

A long-standing resource for those in recovery is the book entitled, *The Recovery Book*, by Al J. Mooney M.D., Catherine Dold, and Howard Eisenberg [12]. This book has been completely revised and updated. It is a classic, chock full of helpful information for those in all stages of recovery. It's very readable, and something you can continually go to for advice and guidance on any number of topics related to recovery. My primary reservation of this excellent work is that despite being updated, it gives mutual support groups, other than A.A., little mention. Many helpful pages are devoted to A.A., but there is little beyond website addresses for important organizations such as SMART Recovery, Secular Organization for Sobriety, Women for Sobriety and other abstinence-based programs. Not surprisingly, there is no mention of the non-abstinence-based Moderation Management program at all.

I believe the time has come to acknowledge these other fine resources and assist clients in selecting support services that most closely align with their values, beliefs, and stage of readiness. I believe we do clients

6 - WILLINGNESS TO CHANGE

a disservice by not helping them to identify a range of options.

It is worth noting that the new edition (2014) of *The Recovery Book* now divides recovery into three recovery zones [12], which are highly compatible with the PDMT Model. The PDMT Model was first published in journal articles in 2006/2007 and then as a book in 2010 [1]. Ironically, the color zones in *The Recovery Book* are identical to the primary colors selected to represent the four paradigms of the PDMT Model, with the addition of the color purple for Paradigm 4 (Transformation).

The similarity in the division of recovery stages (Zones and Paradigms) and the identical color coding makes it easy to utilize both resources with clarity and little confusion. Clients activate their recovery in the Red Zone, which closely parallels themes in the PDMT Paradigm 1; the Yellow Zone is devoted to issues that focus on rebuilding your life in recovery, also the focus of themes in Paradigm 2; the Green Zone represents later recovery issues which correspond to the PDMT themes of ongoing recovery in Paradigms 3 and 4. Utilizing *The Recovery Book* information and activities along with the Paradigm Model themes, guidance, and exercises, provides a comprehensive template for recovery. Combine these resources with any of the reputable mutual support groups in your community and you create a powerful toolbox to address addiction and initiate recovery [12:p.22,23].

REFERENCE LIST

[1] L.G. DiStefano, LCSW and M. Hohman, Ph.D., *The Paradigm Developmental Model of Treatment:*

A Clinical Guide for Counselors Working with Substance Abusers and the Chemically Dependent. San Diego, CA: Montezuma Publishing, 2010.

[2] Alcoholics Anonymous World Services, Inc. (2016, Aug.). *The Twelve Steps of Alcoholics Anonymous* [Online]. Available: http://www.aa.org/assets/en_US/smf-121_en.pdf

[3] The University of Rhode Island, Cancer Research Center. (2017). *Detailed Overview of the Transtheoretical Model of Behavior Change* [Online]. Available: http://web.uri.edu/cprc/detailed-overview/

[4] L.G. DiStefano, LCSW, *The Paradigm Developmental Model of Treatment Group Topics.* San Diego, CA: Montezuma Publishing, 2012.

[5] SMART Recovery. (2017). *SMART Recovery Position Statements* [Online]. Available: www.smartrecovery.org/resources/position.htm

[6] SMART Recovery. (2017). *SMART Recovery— Self-Management for Addiction Recovery* [Online]. Available: www.smartrecovery.org

[7] SMART Recovery. (2017). *Introduction to SMART Recovery* [Online]. Available: www.smartrecovery.org/intro

[8] SMART Recovery. (2017). *Frequently Asked Questions About SMART Recovery* [Online]. Available: http://www.smartrecovery.org/resources/faq.htm#Q. What is the scientific foundation on which SMART Recovery® is built

[9] SMART Recovery (2013, July). *SMART Recovery News and Views.* Volume 19, Issue 3 [Online]. Available: http://www.smartrecovery.org/resources/library/Newsletters/Newsletters/summer-2013-news-and-views.pdf

[10] SMART Recovery. (2016, Mar. 28). SMART Recovery Meetings Cross 2,000 Mark, Including

1,000 in U.S. [Online]. Available: http://www.smartrecovery.org/pressroom/2000thMeeting.pdf

[11] SMART Recovery. (2017). *Smart Recovery Online Shop, Other Languages* [Online]. Available: https://www.smartrecovery.org/shop/products/other-languages/

[12] A.J. Mooney M.D. et al., *The Recovery Book*. New York, NY: Workman Publishing Co. Inc., 2014.

PARADIGM CHANGE

CHAPTER 7

THEME 7
ACTION TO CHANGE

The next paradigm theme (#7) is Action to Change. In cognitive-behavioral therapy, this represents the behavioral piece of the work. First, there is the mental process of thinking about change and deciding to do something. Next, we take action and make that behavioral change. The Paradigm Developmental Model is designed as a cognitive-behavioral approach to treatment. [1]. The PDMT themes, like the Twelve Steps of A.A. are developmental. In other words, first you think and then you do.

Recovery begins to become a reality when a person purposefully corrects, alters, or initiates new behavior that supports their recovery. In the previous chapter we discussed the willingness of several clients to prepare to make a significant change. When they actually took the steps and initiated the change, they moved from willingness into action.

MARILYN'S STORY

The last time I spoke with Marilyn was in preparation for this book, and she was several months away from being 30 years sober. A self-proclaimed alcoholic, Marilyn, an upper-middleclass housewife with three children, first went to A.A. in the late 1980s. Marilyn is Jewish and has no alcoholism in her family history, but a grandparent did have a severe gambling problem.

According to Marilyn, she used alcohol to cope with the stresses and strains of raising three active children. Her husband, although loving, was frequently absent from the home due to his busy medical practice. Marilyn's alcoholism rapidly accelerated when she discovered she had breast cancer and underwent a very difficult radical mastectomy of both breasts. Although the cancer was successfully treated and she eventually was pronounced cancer free, she was caught in a cycle of grief and anger that lasted many years. She will tell you today that she shut her husband out for several years, but at the time she did not understand her reactions. When he finally left, he became involved with a woman who had been a close friend of Marilyn's. This further enraged Marilyn and provided the fuel that drove her into the depths of her disease.

Marilyn found her way to A.A. and despite initial misgivings, she stayed with the program, worked the steps, and developed a support system of women in the program. She has had just two different sponsors over her entire 30 years.

When I question Marilyn today as to what has contributed to her ability to remain clean and sober, she names several things. She desperately wanted to be in the lives of her children and grandchildren. Today, she not only has healthy relationships with her three children but also has seven grandchildren. She had lived in California for some years, but relocated back to New York at the urging of her family to be more involved in their daily lives: a big sign that they trusted her sobriety.

The second factor Marilyn acknowledges is her daily commitment to running. She states that she relishes starting off each day with a run. She recognizes that running stimulates her brain chemistry and that the "high" she experiences supports her sense of well-being. Although Marilyn had been on antidepressant medication in the past, it is no longer necessary.

Marilyn recognizes that her running is somewhat compulsive. She admits that whenever she travels and finds herself in a new situation the first thing she does is figure out where she can have a morning run. Several years ago, she sustained a foot injury that prevented her from exercise. She explains that it was a very difficult time and she was compelled to increase her A.A. program attendance. She was also compelled to learn alternative coping strategies including meditation which has enriched her sobriety and which she continues to practice. Marilyn still attends meetings about twice each month and is involved with newcomers.

Marilyn has put together a strong recovery program that has stood the test of time. She has added components like family therapy and antidepressant medication as she has needed. Her program has grown as she has grown, as evidenced by her service work today. But if you ask Marilyn to pick one component essential to her sobriety, aside from her motivation to keep her family, she will tell you running.

THE ACTIONS OF RECOVERY

Traditional recovery actions to follow:
- Attend support groups/meetings on a predetermined regular schedule
- Talk regularly with a counselor, therapist, and friends in recovery; set up appointments, phone dates, and coffee meetings
- Read up-to-date literature, educate yourself, and share what you've learned; don't forget online web sites and information
- Get rid of alcohol and other drugs in your environment, along with paraphernalia; create a safe zone

7 - ACTION TO CHANGE

- Evaluate your mental health with a professional for a co-occurring disorder if you are experiencing symptoms of depression, anxiety, or other mental health concerns
- Involve your family; ask for their support in creating a sobriety-centered life
- Stop the use of drugs or alcohol under medical supervision; involve your physician in your recovery so medical issues, including medications, can be monitored or addressed: remember to get an annual physical
- Change the people, places, and things that contributed to your alcohol/drug involvement: this should be done as quickly as possible
- Build a recovery support system of friends and coworkers that you trust and can rely on to sustain your sobriety-centered life

Aside from these standard recovery actions, many of my clients have found other actions that have helped anchor their recovery. Marilyn found running to be extremely valuable. Young Bobby found weekly motorcycle trips with a group of recovering bikers and Peggy found game night!

PEGGY'S STORY

Peggy, an articulate go-getter, has many friends and loves to socialize. Unfortunately, alcoholism was very prevalent in her family history, and she was afraid she was on the road to disaster. Peggy was in the very early stages of alcohol use disorder. Under 20 percent of adults with lifetime alcohol use disorder ever seek treatment or ask for help [2]. Peggy, fortunately, had a boyfriend whose deceased father was alcoholic, and consequently, he had a very low tolerance for alcoholic behavior. He did not drink, which made it easy to create a safe home environment. However Peggy, who was in her early 30s, worked for a national clothing chain with young employees who liked to party.

To be truthful, I had doubts that Peggy would be willing to make the changes necessary to remain abstinent so early in her process. Nevertheless, Peggy rejected a moderation approach for herself and dove into recovery with energy and commitment. She tried both SMART Recovery and A.A. She ended up finding a weekly women's A.A. meeting that she loved. It became her home group. She stayed in treatment with me for her first full year of recovery, actively working through the paradigm themes discussed in this book.

A major obstacle for Peggy was the estrangement she felt from friends who consistently invited her to happy hours and other drinking-related activities. While she did attend her company's holiday party and several other work-related events, she steered clear of social activities with work friends that involved drinking, including watching sporting events at bars. She struggled with that one. At first, she thought she could go and just drink club soda or another non-alcoholic beverage, but she soon recognized that the experience made her feel deprived and triggered cravings. Her boyfriend had a best male friend, also in recovery, and the three of them began to watch football games together.

In therapy one day, we were discussing the social isolation she was experiencing when she mentioned that her boyfriend had a gazillion board games that she really enjoyed playing. In that session the concept of "game

7 - ACTION TO CHANGE

night" was born. Peggy decided to host weekly, alcohol-free game nights for friends in recovery and others who understood it was an alcohol-free event. The concept proved to be an amazing antidote to Peggy's social isolation. Every Thursday evening at 7:00pm she and her boyfriend hosted anywhere from six to a dozen people. She introduced a new game each night. She created playing areas around the house for the activities. They purchased a fire pit for the backyard and strung lights on the patio. Peggy would provide various appetizers and nonalcoholic beverages and guests would bring various desserts and snacks. It has been over two years and this event is still going strong. Because of the couple's work schedules, which include weekends, Thursday night is their equivalent of Saturday night. Now their home is filled with laughter, fierce competition, and comradery.

I hope the above story illustrates my point. Nowhere in recovery literature will you read that a game night will help to keep you clean and sober. Nevertheless, it was a very important factor in helping Peggy achieve her first year of recovery. Instead of ruminating about what she couldn't do, she focused on what she could do. What surprised her was that a number of her drinking friends loved game night so much they became regulars at the event. This provided the opportunity to keep and enjoy these friendships in a safe and productive way. All the preparations for game night (cooking, game selection, set up, etc.) kept Peggy fully engaged and provided a chance for both Peggy and her boyfriend to host something together that was meaningful to them both.

THEIR STORIES CONTINUE...

Remember Estella, my client who left her alcoholic husband and relocated to San Diego? One of the actions she took to support and enhance her recovery was to join the Unitarian Universalist Church. This fellowship provided instant friendship and support. They host a large number of social events at her fellowship. She identifies herself as in recovery and has experienced significant support. According to Estella, this church welcomes everyone and is about community. This church provided the proverbial "port in a storm" during Estella's transition to San Diego. It was an action that greatly helped to anchor her recovery and enlarge her support system.

Remember Ron, my client who also has a bipolar mental health condition? After two years of individual therapy focusing on the paradigm themes as they related to his recovery process, he added the action of couples therapy. Ron recognized that his reluctance to engage regularly with a sponsor left him without a source of consistent feedback. While he worked on that issue, he saw the value of providing an opportunity for both he and his wife to discuss home/family topics related to his recovery in counseling. Given Ron's bipolar condition, this proved to be very valuable. On more than one occasion his wife was able to recognize signs that Ron was becoming symptomatic. Quick medication adjustments and supportive counseling stabilized the situations and helped to prevent alcohol relapse.

THE IMPORTANCE OF H.A.L.T. [3]

For many years, the recovery community has provided newcomers with this sage advice: "Never get too Hungry, Angry, Lonely, or Tired" (H.A.L.T.). It makes

7 - ACTION TO CHANGE

perfect sense from a biochemical perspective. Think about it. When we are hungry, we become irritable, cranky, and thin-skinned. These emotions pose a threat to remaining clean and sober. As blood sugar levels drop, high risk increases in a variety of areas. If we are angry, chemicals are rushing through our bodies and serenity is gone. When serenity is lost, we are more vulnerable to relapse triggers. Loneliness can quickly activate the negative committee. An expression in the community is, "poor me, poor me, pour me a drink!" Have you ever seen a tired two-year-old? Reason and logic are gone. When we are tired, we risk the loss of our cognitive defenses.

Most people think of high-risk situations as something external (bars, dealers, sporting events, etc.) While that is true, it is also true that H.A.L.T. problems represent a significant internal high-risk threat.

Therefore, actions that help to prevent H.A.L.T. are paramount to maintaining the emotional balance and biochemistry necessary to foster recovery.

I am not aware of any research proof, but I am convinced after more than 30 years of talking with clients, that people are triggered to relapse because of H.A.L.T. issues more than anything else.

So what actions can reduce the difficulties associated with H.A.L.T.? Following are some examples.

ACTIONS TO MANAGE H.A.L.T.

- Eat healthy meals and snacks four to five times a day. It's important to keep blood-sugar (glucose) levels stable. Hypoglycemia (low blood sugar) can happen suddenly and can be dangerous. Some of the symptoms of hypoglycemia are shaking, sweating, feeling anxious, feeling irritable, dizziness, and hunger. Consult with a doctor immediately if you experience these symptoms [4].

- Take active steps to manage your anger. Counseling, anger management classes, and couples or family therapy can contribute significantly to your efforts at self-regulation. Remember anger triggers the release of toxic chemicals in the body. When you are on a tirade, you are not just venting emotions, you are releasing harmful chemicals in your body that are destabilizing and can trigger relapse. Finding physical releases for your emotions such as regular exercise can also be extremely helpful, as are meditation practices.

- Loneliness can trigger many negative emotions. Individuals need support systems in life, and this is never more important than in recovery. Actions include regular participation in a self-help group, a counseling program, an activity group such as the Sierra Club or a book club. Remember, the negative committee will seize on feelings of loneliness to create a downhill spiral of negative thinking that includes catastrophizing, dwelling on past pain or grievances, and discounting any positives. This strong pessimism and negativity creates a high relapse potential.

- It is of the uppermost importance to be well-rested. Sleep deprivation can lead to a host of chronic health problems. It can seriously interfere with important decision-making abilities. Regular sleep hours and balanced work/life schedules are essential, but they

7 - ACTION TO CHANGE

won't happen on their own. It takes planning, consistent action, and a commitment to your health and well-being.

- Don't wait to be motivated. Take action in each of these areas daily. Once you do something, motivation is often stimulated. Keep your actions small but consistent. Avoid all or nothing responses. Think of running a recovery marathon as opposed to a 50-yard dash. Pacing, endurance, and focus are keys to success.

We will discuss more about these topics when we address the issue of self-regulation later in this book.

SECOND GEAR

Recovery moves into second gear when consistent actions are taken to support the recovery process. Some actions are traditional and can be learned in recovery literature, meetings, and discussions. Others, however, can prove to be equally as valuable to long-term recovery efforts. Utilizing individual therapy to explore and determine actions that will enhance and anchor your recovery can be of great benefit.

As you grow in recovery ask yourself: "What non-alcohol/drug activities give me joy? What activities give me purpose? What activities stimulate my thinking? What activities engage my senses? What activities help me feel good about myself? What activities connect me to others? What activities would be fun to try?"

Skydiving anyone? Exploring these questions can open you to new possibilities and challenges. Recovery definitely does not have to be boring!

S.E.T. THE DAY

S.E.T. is an acronym for a routine that I created many years ago for my clients. I have also practiced it faithfully for years. This routine helps anchor and facilitate daily accountability and positive intention. It's a simple but effective way to launch your day, keep you focused on priorities, put the previous day to bed with serenity and heighten the awareness of your automatic negative committee thoughts.

I have taught this process to many of my clients, and the collective feedback is that it's a very effective way to focus on behavioral growth and self-management.

I suggest you do this routine early each morning, perhaps after meditation or a morning walk. Find a place where you can sit quietly and focus your thoughts. Here is the process:

S = SCHEDULE: Schedule your day and review your commitments. Don't focus solely on work. Include family, social, personal, and self-care commitments. Determine what you can reasonably accomplish and discern your priorities. It may take more than a day to complete a priority/commitment, so are there any from yesterday that will carry over to today, and what are the next steps necessary to move forward? After you're satisfied that you have set and created a reasonable blueprint for the day, focus your attention on E.

Note: please remember that we must be flexible with any schedule we create. Emergencies occur and priorities often need to shift. The schedule you create is not written in stone; instead, it's a blueprint designed to give direction and maintain clarity as you progress through your day.

7 - ACTION TO CHANGE

E = EVALUATE: Evaluate yesterday. What were your successes and accomplishments? What values do you believe you reinforced? What positive behaviors would you like to replicate and which negative behaviors would you like to replace or extinguish? What would you like to have done better or have addressed? Is there anything you can do today to improve your concerns about yesterday? Is there anything you need to fix or resolve? If so, do it today. This helps to keep resentments from growing, shame from consuming you, and regret from distracting you from the here and now. Simply put, it keeps your side of the street emotionally clean. After you feel that you have thoroughly evaluated yesterday, and have moved forward to today whatever needs to be continued or resolved, you are ready to address the final component of this daily routine.

T = THOUGHTS: Monitor your thoughts throughout the day. Catch negative automatic thoughts from your negative committee and challenge them with positive thoughts and actions. Repeat positive thoughts and affirmations frequently to keep you centered and receptive. When difficulties arise and you experience frustrations, use your affirmations to help keep yourself emotionally balanced and relaxed.

Begin this piece by first reviewing yesterday's thoughts, both positive and negative. Can you see a pattern? For example, if you experienced a work delay, did you get frustrated and immediately negative? Replay the scenario in your mind and replace the negative thought with a positive affirmation. Commit yourself to responding in a more constructive fashion the next time a similar incident occurs.

Perhaps your negative committee thoughts were focused on your feelings of incompetence or self-worth. Recognize this false core belief and challenge it. If you legitimately feel there is something to improve, commit to that improvement. Otherwise, recognize that the only purpose of the negative committee is to bring you down and derail your recovery. Reject these thoughts and don't go down the path of self-sabotage. Engaging in weekly cognitive-behavioral therapy can be very helpful if you find that you are battling daily with your "negative committee."

After you have reviewed the previous day's negative thoughts, turn your focus to the positive thoughts you experienced. Take a moment to feel the empowerment and optimism these thoughts generated. Notice any sensations in your body as you do this piece. A sense of well-being and relaxation often occurs. Commit yourself to the continued fostering of positive self-regard.

End this morning routine with saying out loud two or three things you are grateful for in your life today and conclude with an affirmation that speaks to you.

Utilizing a S.E.T. routine each day is a powerful action tool that will strengthen your recovery. Try this tool for at least three months and evaluate your results. I believe that over time you will experience and identify significant improvements that lead to healing and transformation.

LATER STAGE ACTIONS

Successful long-term recovery is not stagnant. As one grows in sobriety, new challenges will present themselves. New tools will be necessary to manage these challenges.

7 - ACTION TO CHANGE

Perhaps you are several years clean and sober, and your teenage son becomes defiant and sarcastic. While SMART Recovery meetings or A.A. might help you maintain your equilibrium, family therapy might be a new tool that you utilize to address issues with your teenage child.

Several years into sobriety, you might still be fixing the financial wreckage you created during your using days. Again, program support is important to maintain your perspective and keep you grounded, but a financial consultation that includes a budget analysis might provide the most insight. According to the "Collective Wisdom" of many of my clients, "THE TENDENCY TO MINIMIZE, DENY, AND FORGET ANY NUMBER OF OBLIGATIONS OR PROBLEMS DOESN'T AUTOMATICALLY END WITH SOBRIETY."

The reaction of putting your head in the sand tends to become a habitual response. It takes focus and commitment to identify problems before they escalate. It takes humility to reach out for help and problem-solve whatever the issue may be. Ongoing recovery requires the ability to self-regulate, a topic we will discuss in a subsequent chapter.

IN SUMMARY

Healthy, productive, sobriety-based actions are essential for lasting recovery. Begin with the basics outlined at the beginning of this chapter. As your sobriety stabilizes, start to consider other additional actions that will enhance your well-being and provide purpose and joy. As you grow in recovery new challenges will emerge. Seek support and try out new tools. Using a tool is an action. Some tools can bolster your ability to communicate. Other tools can help you determine a strategy or approach to solving a problem. Still other tools will help you keep a problem in perspective and avoid catastrophizing the situation.

By being proactive, you will tend to handle problems, when they are small and manageable. As you gain skill in this area you will gain confidence and your problem-solving abilities will strengthen.

FURTHER INFORMATION

WOMEN FOR SOBRIETY, INC.

"We are capable and competent, caring and compassionate, always willing to help another; bonded together in overcoming our addiction [5]."

- Mission: "Women for Sobriety (WFS) is an organization whose purpose is to help all women find their individual path to recovery through discovery of self, gained by shared experiences, hopes, and encouragement with other women in similar circumstances. We are an abstinence-based self-help program for women facing issues of alcohol or drug addiction [6]."

"Women For Sobriety, Inc. (WFS) is a non-profit organization dedicated to helping women overcome alcoholism and other addictions [7]." The organization bases their New Life Program on 13 statements of "positivity that encourage emotional and spiritual

7 - ACTION TO CHANGE

growth... [7]" The program helps women "achieve sobriety and sustain ongoing recovery [7]."

WFS has been providing services to women alcoholics since July 1976. Although membership is small in number compared to SMART Recovery and A.A., you can find WFS self-help groups across the United States, Canada, England, New Zealand, Australia, Ireland, and Finland. According to their website, there are approximately 300 groups around the world. They also have an active online forum, blogs, a bookstore, and conferences.

"WFS is unique in that it is an organization of women for women [6]." WFS offers a variety of recovery tools to strengthen coping skills and enhance emotional and spiritual growth. WFS is a program that promotes abstinence as a goal. Their literature states, "Membership in WFS requires a sincere desire for an abstinent 'New Life' [6]."

Dr. Jean Kirkpatrick started Women for Sobriety. In her autobiography, *Turnabout: New Help for the Woman Alcoholic,* she describes years of struggling with her alcoholism and difficulty connecting with the A.A. program. In her memoir, she shared that "despite suicide attempts, a stay in a psychiatric hospital, and years of excessive drinking," not once was she diagnosed as alcoholic [8]. Jean became sober by using cognitive methods and decided in 1975 to form an organization and design a program.

She recognized that women frequently suffered from low self-esteem, depression, loneliness, and excessive feelings of guilt. In addition, women also may also experience physical and mental abuse, sexual assault, and violence.

Many years ago, when I directed an inpatient chemical dependency program at a San Diego hospital, we decided to conduct a weekly women's group. Prior to this programming, female patients participated only in mixed groups. The differences we observed were remarkable. In the daily mixed group, women rarely discussed physical abuse, sexual assault, or feelings of low self-esteem. However, in the weekly women's group these were regular topics. Clearly, the mixed groups did not provide the safety and intimacy that was needed to discuss such sensitive topics. This was an important learning lesson for me and the other treatment providers. When I opened my outpatient program, Counseling and Recovery Institute (CRI), we remembered this hospital experience and created a comprehensive treatment track devoted exclusively to women. WFS was created and has grown for similar reasons. It provides a much-needed service for women in recovery.

WFS relates that when Jean appeared on *The Phil Donahue Show* in 1978, they received 500 letters a day for a solid week. Women were grateful to Jean for telling their story. Prior to that appearance, in 1976 *Woman's Day Magazine* ran the article "When A Woman Drinks Too Much," and WFS received thousands of letters from women suffering from their relationship with alcohol [9].

On June 19, 2000, Dr. Jean Kirkpatrick passed away at the age of 77. Her contributions to the recovery community have been enormous. She leaves a rich legacy and a very respected women's program. Thousands of women are gratefully in her debt. Check the WFS website for an abundance of information [9].

REFERENCE LIST

[1] L.G. DiStefano, LCSW and M. Hohman, Ph.D., *The Paradigm Developmental Model of Treatment: A Clinical Guide for Counselors Working with Substance Abusers and the Chemically Dependent.* San Diego, CA: Montezuma Publishing, 2010.

[2] C. Bergland. (2015, June). *What Are the Eleven Symptoms of Alcohol Use Disorder?* [Online]. Available: www.PsychologyToday.com/blog/the-athletes-way/201506/what-are-the-eleven-symptoms-alcohol-use-disorder

[3] Dr. John. (1971, Feb.). *The Essence of AA - H.A.L.T.* [Online]. Available: http://sobertransitions.org/Halt.html

[4] R. Nall, RN, BSN, CCRN, and E. Cirino. (2016, Aug.). *Low Blood Sugar (Hypoglycemia).* [Online]. Available: https://www.healthline.com/health/hypoglycemia#overview1

[5] Women For Sobriety, Inc. (2016). *Group Info* [Online]. Available: http://womenforsobriety.org/beta2/group-info/

[6] WFS Board of Directors. (2011, June 10). *About WFS* [Online] Available: http://womenforsobriety.org/beta2/about-wfs/

[7] Women For Sobriety, Inc. (2016). *Homepage* [Online]. Available: http://www.womenforsobriety.org/beta2/

[8] J. Kirkpatrick, Ph.D., *Turnabout: New Help for the Woman Alcoholic.* Fort Lee, NJ: Barricade Books, Inc., 1977.

[9] Women For Sobriety, Inc. (1999). *Profile of Jean Kirkpatrick, Ph.D.* [Online]. Available: http://www.womenforsobriety.org/wfs_jean.html

PARADIGM CHANGE

CHAPTER 8

THEME 8
ACCOUNTABILITY AND THE GROWTH OF EMPATHY

PARADIGM CHANGE

The eighth paradigm theme pertains to both Accountability and Empathy [1]. Let's begin with the concept of accountability. In Theme #5 we spoke of taking full and complete responsibility for one's recovery. Breaking that theme down further, we come to the notion of accountability.

Think of accountability as being tied to specific actions and behaviors. In Alcoholics Anonymous, Step Eight focuses on amends [2]. In recovery, one begins to contemplate who they may have harmed or hurt and if they are willing to make amends to those people.

Accountability begins with focusing on healing relationships and righting wrongs. It requires an honest appraisal of your behavior toward others and the impact your alcohol or drug abuse had on family, friends, and work environments.

The PDMT theme of accountability goes further. It's important to establish accountability checks and tools. In early recovery, for example, a person might take Antabuse to help with their accountability or volunteer to make coffee at a meeting. A person may agree to weekly family therapy or regular meetings with a sponsor or support person. All of these things will enhance accountability. If a person wants to focus on improving their job performance, they might request a monthly meeting with their supervisor to ensure they are on track and performing to expectations. If a person wants to lose weight in a healthy manner, they might hire a trainer or join a gym to facilitate accountability in this area.

As a person grows in recovery, the tools and checks they use will change, but the notion that accountability is fundamental to ongoing success is what is constant.

8 - ACCOUNTABILITY AND THE GROWTH OF EMPATHY

ACCOUNTABILITY TOOLS

In addition to weekly therapy, the clients we have discussed increased their accountability with the following tools:
- *Ray, Ron,* and *Janet,* the flight attendant, all used Antabuse in early recovery to help them to be accountable and manage urges and cravings.
- *Brian* moved to a supervised recovery home to avoid being alone in early sobriety.
- *Estella* spoke daily with her sponsor regardless of how she felt. She built this accountability measure into her daily routine.
- *Claude* participated in couple's therapy, as did *Ray* and *Ron*, to provide his spouse with an opportunity to provide feedback in a supportive setting and improve his accountability.
- *Bobby* went on weekly motorcycle rides with A.A./NA friends and enjoyed the mentorship they provided over coffee.
- *Peggy* told specific friends at work that she was in recovery and asked for their support as a way to strengthen her accountability. *Ron* did the same.

In addition, all of these clients looked at their guilt, resentments, and emotional pain. Those involved in A.A. working with their sponsor made a list of people they harmed and made amends. Other clients working in therapy decided to whom they might want to apologize and what behavior going forward they wanted to correct. The process of both cleaning up your past regrets and establishing behavioral checks to foster future personal accountability provides a great deal of emotional relief and freedom.

I liken the process to cleaning a street. First, you remove the rubbish, sweep the street, and fix any potholes. After you are satisfied that you have done all you can with the cleanup, you move to the next stage. Now you install stop signs, streetlights, and road markers to help you navigate these streets. This two-part process provides thorough accountability. If you do the first stage (clean-up) without the second, you remain at high risk to repeat the errors that created your guilt and resentment in the first place. If you do only the second stage, you will be building on a damaged foundation. It is very likely that the guilt or resentment will eventually come to the surface and destroy what you wanted to create.

AN EMPLOYEE

During my tenure as the Executive/Clinical Director of the San Diego State University's Driving Under the Influence Program, I had the privilege of working with many counselors who themselves were in recovery. One afternoon I was reading in my office when I heard a commotion. One of our counselors was furious with some administrative glitch and was loudly and angrily complaining to staff. I sat back in my chair as this was an excellent counselor who worked a strong program of recovery. I shook my head, and said to myself, "I guess she's going to be cleaning this up."

Sure enough, the following day I hear this counselor making amends for her outburst. She took full responsibility for the outburst and was accountable for her behavior. The glitch was annoying and time consuming but as she said, "it did not warrant an end-of-the-world tirade."

I interacted with dozens of individuals in recovery over my 14 years as Director. It was evident when a person was "working their program." It didn't mean they were perfect, or didn't have a bad day. But it did mean that they reflected on their interactions with others and, where appropriate, were accountable for their behavior. They were usually the first to admit an error and have a plan to fix the problem in the future.

One of the most endearing examples of accountability happened at my retirement party. As guests were coming into the facility, a former employee made his way over to me. He had been very ill and had made a great effort to attend the party. What makes this story so special was his reason for attending.

He gave me a bear hug, and thrust a card into my hand that read, "To the best boss I ever had." I looked at him with a puzzled expression. He grinned broadly and said, "I know you fired me, but you had to and I deserved it. I broke the rules and you had to do your job. I know how disappointed I made you. I really am sorry. You will always be my favorite boss."

This thoughtful man had taken complete accountability for his actions and had made a heartfelt amend. This was a priceless gift to receive.

ACCOUNTABILITY AND RELAPSE PREVENTION

The highly acclaimed addiction expert and prolific author, Terry Gorski, is a pioneer in the development of relapse prevention. He was the first to develop a list of relapse warning signs. He helped foster the recognition that relapse is not something that just happens but rather is preceded by specific thoughts from the negative committee and risky behaviors [3].

RAY'S STORY CONTINUES...

In the early months of working with Ray and his wife Lynn, I taught him the new concept of relapse prevention and warning signs that Gorski was teaching in California in the mid-1980s. In addition to this, one of the behavioral agreements that Ray made was that before he took that first drink he would call his sponsor or me. He could drink if he wanted to but first he must make the call.

Around 2:00 am one morning my phone rang. It was my answering service (this is an old story!); they said Ray was on the line. They put him through. I heard, "Georgi, Georgi, I think I'm having a relapse." I made the mistake of asking Ray where he was. He became indignant. "You didn't tell me where to call you from; you just told me to call you before I took a drink." I calmed him down and got the story.

He and his wife had an argument, and he left the house and went to what had been his favorite bar. He was angry and gulped down several drinks. But the drinks were non-alcoholic because he still was taking Antabuse and he knew he had to wait a few days. His wife later told me that the bartender said he was furious that he couldn't have alcohol, but was fortunately afraid of the reaction he would have. Upon leaving the bar, he went to the bank and withdrew a large amount of money. He took a cab to the airport and flew to Las Vegas. Once he settled into his room he decided to make the call.

8 - ACCOUNTABILITY AND THE GROWTH OF EMPATHY

Take a moment, and consider his behaviors. Ray's actions were a classic relapse dynamic pattern:
- *He became angry and couldn't deal with his emotions.*
- *He went to the bar to drink, but Antabuse kept him from the alcohol.*
- *Nevertheless, he went to the bank and withdrew money.*
- *He flew to Vegas, which is where in the past he would go on "benders" for days.*

We interrupted Ray's relapse with two tools, the most powerful being the medication Antabuse. The second being his agreement to make the call. Ray never drank alcohol nor gambled during this relapse dynamic, but as you can see, the other behaviors were identical to what he had done for years during his drinking sprees. Ray's sponsor picked him back up at the airport and both he and his wife came in for a session to discuss the incident.

It was a valuable learning experience for Ray. He gained a much greater understanding of his anger and the role it could play in relapse. He could clearly see his relapse pattern and the couple learned more about their communication styles.

I have told Ray's story for many years in training seminars because it so clearly demonstrates the dysfunctional behaviors (signs) that precede the taking of alcohol/drugs. An important aspect of accountability is understanding your relapse triggers and vulnerabilities and managing those factors on a consistent basis. If anger management is an issue, tools like Antabuse can be an important safeguard, as can counseling and classes that address that issue.

EMPATHY

The second part of the eighth theme concerns the development of empathy. This is an extremely vital component to lasting recovery.

Empathy is defined in the dictionary as "the ability to understand and share the feelings of another [4]." An important factor in emotional growth is the ability to be empathic to others. The expression of compassion is a vital ingredient.

Lives that revolve around drug and alcohol use become unbalanced, judgment becomes compromised, communication is minimized, and entitlement tends to grow. As we develop emotionally in recovery, so should our empathic responses, i.e., the ability to see something from another person's point of view. Empathy contributes to the growth of consciousness. When we respond empathically with compassion, our awareness shifts, effecting our paradigms, and consequently the experiences of life become viewed from a new perspective.

An important distinction is the difference between empathy and codependency. The dictionary defines codependency as "excessive emotional or psychological reliance on a partner; typically a partner who requires support due to an illness or addiction [5]." Think of codependency as an unhealthy or dysfunctional way of enabling another person to continue with their drug addiction, alcoholism, or other problem. Typically, codependent thinking and behavior is focused excessively on another person. These relationships tend

8 - ACCOUNTABILITY AND THE GROWTH OF EMPATHY

to be enmeshed. "Codependency is characterized by sacrificing one's personal needs in order to try to meet the needs of others... [6]"

Therefore, while empathy is a healthy and positive attribute in human interaction, codependency can lead to a variety of negative feelings and emotions including intense and unstable interpersonal relationships, over-controlling behaviors, low self-worth, chronic feelings of emptiness, and an overwhelming desire for acceptance and affection [7].

ALONSO'S STORY

Alonso came to therapy a number of years ago. He was struggling in early recovery. He was estranged from his wife who suffered from periodic depression and had two small sons. He desperately did not want to lose his family and tried to save his marriage in marital therapy. When that failed and his wife proceeded with a divorce, he came to see me because he was afraid he would relapse.

Alonso worked very hard. Despite his extensive responsibilities with his children and crazy work hours, he frequently went to A.A. meetings during the week and worked intensely with a sponsor. He was able to stabilize his situation. He moved into his father's home and shared custody with his ex-wife, remaining very active with his children. I saw him through the divorce process and soon after, he decided to complete therapy. He had a strong program in place and a good extended family support system.

Several years passed and Alonso contacted me again. During our first session, he was happy to report that he was three years clean and sober and still involved in the A.A. fellowship. He continued to live with his father, but had gained residential custody of his children due to his ex-wife suffering from severe depression. She had been hospitalized and also attended an outpatient program for depression.

Then Alonso dropped the "proverbial bomb." After his ex-wife's last hospitalization, she had lost her job. She could no longer afford her apartment and her only option was to go to live with her parents in the Midwest. She was reluctant to leave her children, but that appeared to be the only option, at least temporarily. However, Alonso came to the rescue!

He offered for her to live with him and the boys at his father's home. Despite his father's vocal reservations, Alonso pushed a plan into place. He convinced his ex-wife, despite her severe depression, to try and reconcile. She could live with them and get better. It was Alonso's hope that once her depression lifted she would be able to re-engage with him. He had never wanted his family to be broken up and saw this as an opportunity to reunite.

Alonso came to see me at the urging of his sponsor because his plan was unraveling. His ex-wife remained depressed and aloof. They would have sex occasionally, but Alonso felt it was meant to pacify him. He would frequently go to events or activities with their boys by himself. She would spend the day sleeping and did little around the house. The couple returned to couples therapy with their former therapist. Alonso was angry that his ex-wife could not commit to their relationship. She didn't say yes, but she didn't say no. Her ambivalence drove him crazy.

Alonso had a very difficult time understanding that many of his behaviors were codependent and willful. He

8 - ACCOUNTABILITY AND THE GROWTH OF EMPATHY

never accepted their divorce, his wife's lack of interest in a sexual relationship, or the fact that she was suffering from a debilitating depression. Alonso was not being kind and empathic, but rather manipulative. His wife was vulnerable and desperate. She didn't want to leave her children, so his offer was something she agreed to. Apparently she tried to gently let Alonso know (in their couples therapy), that her depression made it difficult to feel anything and that she wanted to be honest with him. She said she needed time to sort out how she felt and didn't want to make false promises. Alonso tried to be tolerant for short bursts of time, but his need for acceptance by her and sexual engagement created intense power struggles and great disappointment.

Slowly, the ex-wife's depression improved, and a former employer offered her a job. It took all of her energy to mobilize and complete a full day of work. She was able to do little for the children or the household. The holiday season was approaching. Alonso begrudgingly acknowledged that his plan hadn't worked.

I pointed out that had he been a friend to his ex-wife and offered her a place to recuperate with no strings attached, that would have been truly empathic. He would be helping the mother of his children and someone for whom he cared. However, he pushed the reconciliation of the marriage from day one. She was not in a healthy enough place to make that kind of decision. I did acknowledge that the children were able to see their mother daily and that she was able to recuperate and obtain a job. These were things he could feel good about providing. I suggested that going forward they bank her money, so that if they didn't reunite she would have the funds to get a place nearby. If they did stay together, the money could be used to leave his father's home and get a place of their own. Alonso had a great deal of difficulty accepting the situation. He said he was out of patience and that they needed to make a decision right after the holidays. He dropped out of therapy soon after.

It is not surprising or unusual for someone to want to keep their family together. However, Alonso did not want to be emotionally abandoned by his ex-wife and manipulated the situation to entice her to return to his home. That action further increased her depression and sense of guilt and remorse. Alonso did care for his ex-wife; nevertheless, many of his actions were extremely codependent. He made appointments for her, monitored her schedule, and decided what they would do on weekends. The couple's therapist worked to help the ex-wife take responsibility for her life and express her feelings, but she was afraid that Alonso would get angry and throw her out of the house. She didn't want to leave her children, so she remained compliant and depressed.

Alonso didn't like it when his sponsor confronted him about his underlying motives. He dropped this insightful sponsor and not long after dropped out of therapy. His extreme codependency and willfulness made him feel like a victim.

At the end of the day, it wasn't true empathy for his ex-wife that motivated Alonso, but rather codependency. These issues and the feelings of victimization made him a potential risk for relapse. It should be clarified that a person with a chemical dependency can also be the person with a codependency. In this case, the ex-wife had an illness (depression) and the recovering alcoholic (Alonso) was also codependent.

8 - ACCOUNTABILITY AND THE GROWTH OF EMPATHY

ALONSO UPDATE

Alonso had dropped out of therapy for a little over six months. One day I received this touching text, "Hi Georgi, I helped Janice move out yesterday. I'm still sober, still a dad very positive, and a big chunk of the courage and honesty to make that decision came with your help. You kept my eyes open to a picture I didn't always want to look at. A very heartfelt thank you." Alonso has returned to weekly therapy and is moving on with his life. The final separation from his ex-wife was a very painful experience, but he has remained sober and has learned a great deal about himself in the process. Over time, he demonstrated a remarkable amount of courage and honesty and the ability to recognize "his self will run riot."

THE DEER IN NARA

Over the years I have made a number of trips to Japan to train social workers, nurses, physicians, and other healthcare professionals in chemical dependency treatment. In the 1990s, we utilized translators whenever I would lecture. I found that trying to explain codependency was a very difficult undertaking. Japan is a very different culture, and the traditional role of women involved a high degree of care-taking. Despite distinct variables, however, there is a spectrum of behavior that is considered healthy and appropriate in most cultures.

I was scheduled to speak in Osaka in June 1993 and was worried that codependency would be a hard concept to explain. It was particularly difficult because people assumed that if you no longer had contact with the alcoholic, you would no longer be codependent. I struggled with trying to determine how best to present these concepts.

Before I arrived in Osaka, my hosts and I stopped for a day of rest and relaxation in the ancient city of Nara. Nara is a very beautiful small city with a large public park. Over 1,000 deer freely roam the park. In those days vendors sold pancake-shaped cookies for visitors to feed the deer. My always-gracious hosts purchased a handful of cookies for me to feed the deer. Gingerly, I held out a cookie to a deer and quite unconsciously, I bowed my head. Head bowing is a constant gesture in Japan, and after two weeks it had become routine. The deer absolutely surprised me by bowing back! That's correct, the deer actually bowed its head as it ate the cookie! My hosts started to laugh at our interaction. I fed several more deer, and they all responded in a similar fashion. As I looked around I realized that the great majority of visitors to the park were Japanese. They all bowed their heads when they offered a deer a cookie and the deer responded in kind. It was a fun afternoon but I didn't think any more about it.

As I was giving my lecture in Osaka it came back to me. I told the audience the experience with the deer in Nara. They all laughed with recognition. I explained that I have a sister who lived at the time in northern New Jersey. Each winter the deer would come down the mountain in search of food. I asked the audience, "what if we took a dozen deer from Nara and flew them to my sister's backyard in Northern New Jersey? If I came out of the house with cookies and bowed to the deer, would the deer bow back?"

After a moment of laughter from the crowd I said "yes, they would." Another round of laughter. Why?

8 - ACCOUNTABILITY AND THE GROWTH OF EMPATHY

Because they had been conditioned to bow back. I explained that the same is true for codependency. You can get divorced and marry a different person or move many miles away. Unless you address the conditioning that has occurred over possibly many years, your reactions will remain similar. I often joke that if I had a penny for every time I heard, "I didn't think my second husband or wife was also alcoholic when I married them," I would be a millionaire.

It is not an accident that a person selects a relationship with similar dynamics. That is why it's so important to address your codependency issues, whether you are still in a relationship or not.

FURTHER INFORMATION

SECULAR ORGANIZATIONS FOR SOBRIETY (SOS)

Secular Organizations for Sobriety is an anonymous support group for those seeking sobriety by way of a secular path. They offer a variety of resources, including both printed and video materials, to assist new groups in forming and remaining in alignment with SOS principals.

"SOS empowers the individual to find and keep sobriety and or abstinence [8]." According to their literature, SOS members are welcome to share experiences, insights, information, strength, and encouragement in supportive group meetings. SOS is self-supporting and refuses outside funding. It's an abstinence-based program. "Sobriety is the number one priority in a recovering person's life. As such, he or she must abstain from all drugs or alcohol [9]."

"SOS encourages the scientific study of addiction in all its aspects. SOS does not limit its outlook to one area of knowledge or theory of addiction [9]."

James Christopher founded SOS in 1985. James became sober in 1978 and felt a need to provide resources to secular alcoholics. The film, *No God at the Bottom of a Glass,* tells the story of James Christopher and the creation of SOS. It won a 2014 Telly Award. It also was an official selection at the International Freethought Film Festival in Ontario Canada in 2016. James Christopher has written two books on addiction. His book, *SOS Sobriety* distinguishes the SOS model as an alternative to the 12-step model [10].

SOS's headquarters are located in Hollywood, California. According to the organization's website, meetings now span the globe.

"SOS is a non-profit network of autonomous, non-professional local groups, dedicated solely to helping individuals achieve and maintain sobriety/abstinence from alcohol and drug addiction, food addiction and other compulsive behaviors [10]."

SOS has stood the test of time. It reached 32 years as an active organization in 2017. Today, there are group meetings in many cities throughout the world. In addition, dozens of online groups utilize the principles of SOS. The organization has put out this statement, which speaks volumes about its place in the recovery community: "SOS respects recovery in any form, regardless of the path by which it is achieved. It is not opposed to or in competition with any other recovery program [11]."

REFERENCE LIST

[1] L.G. DiStefano, LCSW and M. Hohman, Ph.D., *The Paradigm Developmental Model of Treatment: A Clinical Guide for Counselors Working with Substance Abusers and the Chemically Dependent.* San Diego, CA: Montezuma Publishing, 2010.

[2] Alcoholics Anonymous World Services, Inc. (2016, Aug.). *The Twelve Steps of Alcoholics Anonymous* [Online]. Available: http://www.aa.org/assets/en_US/smf-121_en.pdf

[3] T. T. Gorski and M. Miller, *Staying Sober: A Guide for Relapse Prevention.* Independence, MO: Herald House—Independence Press, 1986, ch. 8, p. 5.

[4] Oxford University Press: English Oxford Living Dictionaries. (2017). *empathy* [Online]. Available: https://en.oxforddictionaries.com/definition/us/empathy

[5] Oxford University Press: English Oxford Living Dictionaries. (2017). *codependency* [Online]. Available: https://en.oxforddictionaries.com/definition/us/codependency

[6] GoodTherapy.com. (2015, Nov. 13). *Therapy for Codependency* [Online]. Available: www.goodtherapy.org/learn-about-therapy/issues/codependency

[7] Wikipedia. (2017, Oct. 9). *Codependency* [Online]. Available: https://en.wikipedia.org/w/index.php?title=Codependency&oldid=804505971

[8] Secular Organizations for Sobriety (SOS). (2016). *What We Do* [Internet]. Available: http://www.sossobriety.org/what-we-do

[9] Secular Organizations for Sobriety (SOS). (2016). *General Principles of SOS* [Online]. Available: https://static1.squarespace.com/static/576740f45016e10f9510a056/t/5768d296893fc08c1a44efc4/1466487450589/SOS_Principles.pdf
[10] Secular Organizations for Sobriety, (SOS). (2016). *About Us* [Online]. Available: http://www.sossobriety.org
[11] Secular Organizations for Sobriety (SOS). (2016). *About Jim Christopher* [Online]. Available: http://www.sossobriety.org/jim-christopher

PARADIGM 3
SELF-REGULATION

PARADIGM CHANGE

CHAPTER 9

THEME 9
FORGIVENESS AND ACCEPTING CONSEQUENCES

PARADIGM 3: SELF-REGULATION

The ninth theme, Forgiveness and Accepting Consequences, initiates the third paradigm of the PDMT Model. The third paradigm contains three themes and represents the quality and longevity associated with long-term recovery.

In this paradigm, cognitive/behavioral processes start to become fully integrated and internalized by the individual. The themes associated with this section reflect the deeper self-understanding and accountability that occurs in later recovery when self-regulation is an active daily process. Individuals have taken responsibility for their recovery, built on their strengths, and actively manage any self-defeating behavior. Individuals at this stage have mastered the ability to self-correct, have adopted positive health practices, and engage in advanced relapse prevention planning. Mindfulness practices focus the individual in the here and now and promote an appreciation for authentic living. [1]

THEME 9: ASKING FORGIVENESS - ACCEPTING CONSEQUENCES

According to the Twelve Steps of A.A., when an alcoholic or addict becomes accountable and recognizes they have injured someone, they make amends to that person [2]. The core theme of this activity is asking for forgiveness and accepting consequences that might occur from this action. One of the most powerful human interactions occurs when a person acknowledges the injury they have caused another and is forgiven. This usually becomes a very healing experience for both parties.

9 - FORGIVENESS AND ACCEPTING CONSEQUENCES

What is forgiveness? The dictionary defines it as a "conscious, deliberate decision to release feelings of resentment or vengeance toward a person or group who you believe has harmed you [3]." Forgiveness does not mean that you minimize or forget the seriousness of an offense against you. It also does not obligate you to continue a relationship, reconcile, or release someone from legal accountability. Instead, forgiveness frees the forgiver from living with corrosive anger [3].

Forgiveness involves letting go of deeply-held negative feelings. Negative feelings are the lifeblood of the negative committee. Releasing negative feelings is essential to sustained and lasting recovery. It's virtually impossible to live in serenity, equilibrium, and mindfulness if our mind and heart are experiencing the toxic effects of constant anger, resentment, hatred, or vengefulness. That is a formula for continuous relapse, so it is essential in recovery to rid oneself of those negative emotions.

Simply said, we cannot afford resentments in recovery. "Collective Wisdom" tells us that "IT DOES NOT MATTER IF THE RESENTMENT IS BIG OR SMALL." If it becomes our focus and stirs negative emotions, it becomes a danger to remaining clean and sober.

ACCEPTING CONSEQUENCES

It is important to prepare for the fact that someone may refuse to accept your apology, or they may accept your apology but not be willing to continue a relationship. We might see this dynamic in family of origin situations. For example, an alcoholic parent may ask an adult child for forgiveness of their behavior. The adult child may acknowledge the gesture but not be willing to resume an active relationship. Siblings may also not want to reconcile with a brother or sister with a drug addiction.

Often feelings of grief, shame, and loss accompany this type of rejection. Working with a counselor or a support person can be invaluable during these times. It's important to focus on what you can control and understand what you cannot. It's in your control to ask for forgiveness. It's in your control to change your behavior moving forward. However, you cannot control the reaction to your apology.

Before asking for forgiveness from someone, think through the possible responses you might get. Prepare yourself emotionally by trying to see things from the other person's perspective. Understand that the person you are dealing with might not understand the disease of alcoholism or the complexities of addiction. There may be other variables you might need to consider. For example, a sibling may have a spouse who adamantly does not want you around their children or extended family. Work through the various reactions in your mind and emotionally acknowledge the grief, shame, and loss that might accompany these reactions. After you have prepared for the action of asking for forgiveness from someone, go ahead and do it unless it would be harmful or detrimental to them.

The "Collective Wisdom" I have heard over and over is that "THE ACT OF ASKING FOR FORGIVENESS PROVIDES A TREMENDOUS AMOUNT OF RELIEF AND SERENITY."

FORGIVING SELF

Perhaps the hardest person to forgive is yourself. Over the years, my clients have struggled with acute

9 - FORGIVENESS AND ACCEPTING CONSEQUENCES

guilt and shame regarding their behavior toward family, friends, and work colleagues. They often look back, with profound regret, at the things they said and did while actively using.

In therapy, however, they learn that the negative committee will seize upon their distress and use their guilt and shame against them. They come to understand that negative emotions set the stage for relapse and that it's fundamental to acknowledge, grieve, and release those negative emotions as expeditiously as possible. We cannot change the past or minimize the devastating impact we may have had on others. Nevertheless, we can go forward with humility and self-management so that the future is not destined to be a repeat of the past.

As an individual works through the themes of the PDMT Model, they grow in self-understanding and self-regulation. When a person replaces corrosive anger, resentment, and negativity with acceptance, love, and unconditional regard, they create a mental and emotional inner world that nurtures recovery. This inner peace is supported and sustained by acts of generosity to self and others.

NELSON MANDELA MODELS FORGIVENESS

There is perhaps no greater example to explain the power of forgiveness or demonstrate its remarkable healing effects than to understand the life of Nelson Mandela. I have included his story here not only because it's inspirational, but because it is instructive. We can learn much about the concepts of recovery (in the broadest sense of the word) from learning about how this man's choices, in the face of grave hardship, led to healing and transformation on the most profound level.

Nelson Mandela was not a saint. He was a human being who experienced fear, anger, abuse, hostility, degradation, and incredible injustice. Nevertheless, he systematically challenged his negative thinking, opened his heart, and practiced forgiveness on a daily basis. His focus on affirmative actions fought despair, and not only kept his heart open but also opened the closed hearts of others. By living his life with grace, optimism, and purpose, he transcended the confines of his jail and infused a civil rights movement leading a nation to significant historical change.

Whenever your recovery becomes difficult, the challenges become great, or the pain becomes overwhelming, think of this man. Whenever you are ambivalent about an act of forgiveness, think of this man. Thinking of him will help put your current challenge in perspective. Adjusting and balancing our perspective is an important cognitive recovery tool.

THE POWER OF FORGIVENESS

Nelson Mandela was born Rolihlahla Mandela on July 18, 1918. On his very first day of school, his primary school teacher gave him the name Nelson, as was the racist custom with black children. He grew up in South Africa, a country that supported extreme segregation between whites and blacks known as apartheid. The government rigorously enforced regulations on the lives of black South Africans. In 1952, Mandela became the National Volunteer-in-Chief of the Campaign for Defiance of Unjust Laws. That same year, he and Oliver Tambo started South Africa's first black law firm, Mandela and Tambo [4]

9 - FORGIVENESS AND ACCEPTING CONSEQUENCES

Mandela was first convicted and sent to prison for leaving the country illegally and encouraging a strike. In 1962, he and and seven other members of the African National Congress (ANC) were arrested for conspiring to overthrow the state and sentenced to life imprisonment at hard labor [5].

Nelson Mandela served 27 years in prison. He spent the first 18 years of his sentence on Robben Island, a bleak and barren region off the coast of Cape Town. He spent the remainder of his sentence at Pollsmoor Maximum Security Prison and then Victor Verster Prison [5].

Mandela experienced the harshest conditions early in his incarceration. Designated a Class D prisoner, he could only receive one visitor and one letter every six months. His cell was a damp, eight-foot by seven-foot concrete slab with a straw mattress and a few flimsy blankets [6] [7]. Mandela suffered daily disappointments and humiliations. He experienced countless emotional and physical hardships, such as when prison authorities abruptly ended his educational studies [6] and regularly forced him to bathe with buckets of frigid Atlantic seawater [7]. While in prison, both his mother and eldest son died, but he was not allowed to attend their funerals [4].

WHY FORGIVENESS WAS HIS STRONGEST DEFENSE

A constant state of coercive anger, resentment, and hatred will erode physical strength, thought clarity, and the body's natural defenses. Mandela was smart enough to recognize that he could not afford toxic resentment if he was going to survive. It was in prison, in the most dire of circumstances, that he began his remarkable journey toward forgiveness of his enemies and reconciliation [5].

The United Nations Security Council called for Mandela's release in 1980. He was finally released in February 1990, nine days after the government officially accepted the ANC as a political party in South Africa. Mandela was heralded as a hero throughout the world for his commitment to human rights and his resilience in the face of terrible oppression. In 1993, he shared the Nobel Peace Prize with President F.W. de Klerk "For their work for the peaceful termination of the apartheid regime, and for laying the foundations for a new democratic South Africa [8]."

USING FORGIVENESS TO HELP HIS NATION HEAL

In May 1994, Nelson Mandela led his ANC party to victory and became South Africa's first democratically elected President. He was also their first black President. His government concentrated on "dismantling the legacy of apartheid by tackling institutionalized racism and fostering racial reconciliation" [6].

Mandela led by example. He reconciled and forgave individuals who had been his jailers during captivity. He demonstrated the power of forgiveness in several acts of humility and grace [9].

On the 20th anniversary of his release from prison, he invited Christo Brand, his primary prison guard at Robben Island, to a celebratory dinner. When asked why he invited Brand, he responded by reflecting on their relationship over the years.

"It reinforced my belief in the essential humanity of even those who had kept me behind bars [9]." In 1995, he had dinner with the State Prosecutor Percy Yutar, who

9 - FORGIVENESS AND ACCEPTING CONSEQUENCES

had demanded the death penalty in his 1993 conviction. "Mandela said that Yutar had only been doing his job [9]."

TEACHES A NATION

Despite these personal acts of forgiveness and reconciliation, Mandela recognized his country was precariously on the edge of what could have been a disastrous civil war. Many white South Africans were afraid they would lose their land, resources, and quality of life. He knew he needed to do something symbolic to bring the country together and foster reconciliation [10].

Few symbols epitomized oppression for Mandela, the ANC, and their membership, more than the hated green and gold jersey of the Springboks, the South African National Rugby Team. At home matches, black South Africans were made to stand in "pens." There was even an international Rugby boycott imposed on South Africa because of their dehumanizing apartheid practices [9].

Mandela made a deliberate and well-thought-out decision of how to address these issues that threatened their new democracy. He began by developing a relationship with Francois Pienaar, the famous and well-regarded captain of the Springboks Rugby team. Mandela believed that Rugby could help heal the nation's racial divisions. However, he recognized that South African blacks cheered for whatever opponent played their national team [10].

He enlisted Pienaar in his belief that winning the World Cup could unite the blacks and whites of South Africa. What followed was well documented in the 2008 book, *Playing the Enemy: Nelson Mandela and The Game that Made a Nation* [10]. The story was so compelling that the following year Clint Eastwood made the Academy Award-nominated film *Invictus*. The movie is a biographical sports drama about the events in South Africa before and during the 1995 hosting of the World Cup, which was hosted in that country following the end of apartheid [11].

Before the final game, the Springboks team, led by Pienaar, visited Robben Island where Mandela spent the first 18 years of his imprisonment. Pienaar was incredibly inspired by Mandela and stated after the prison visit, "Mandela could spend almost 30 years in a tiny cell and come out ready to forgive the people who put him there [11]." The film captures Mandela's dramatic walk onto the stadium field, dressed in a green and gold jersey with Pienaar's number stenciled on the back. He waved his cap to the crowd, and they responded with a thunderous ovation. Pienaar remembers that at that moment, he knew Mandela had become South Africa's true leader. He delivered a moving and heartfelt tribute to Mandela after the World Cup final [7].

The moving story of Nelson Mandela so clearly demonstrates the power of forgiveness. Rather than being broken in prison, he learned on a daily basis how to overcome negative and hostile emotions and to look for and nurture small acts of humanity and decency. He took those strengths and skills and helped a nation emerge from an entrenched, institutionalized state of racism to a functional democracy.

Nelson Mandela died on December 5, 2013 at the age of 95. His death was acknowledged and mourned around the world. His legacy lives on. [6]

9 - FORGIVENESS AND ACCEPTING CONSEQUENCES

CLIENTS AND FORGIVENESS

RAY'S STORY CONTINUES...

Ray is the client I spoke about in the beginning of this book. He spent years in a progressive disease process, unable to control his drinking and unwilling to get help until he was in the later stages of his addiction. Fortunately, by working together over time, Ray developed a strong program of recovery. However, about two years into Ray's sobriety, both he and I knew that he had to deal with his feelings of anger and rage toward his mother.

Ray's mother was a prostitute. She also drank and took various pills to get high. Most hurtful to Ray was that she was completely inattentive, even when not working. Ray remembered feelings of tremendous loneliness and neglect.

I recognized that Ray could not tolerate a deep surgical exploration of his childhood. A supportive emotional catharsis that felt safe and connected to his spiritual beliefs might provide a needed release of his repressed emotions. His sobriety was stable, but his childhood was like walking through an emotional minefield. So rather than delve into the specifics of numerous painful childhood memories, we instead acknowledged his difficult childhood and the tremendous pain it caused and focused our work on forgiveness and his personal healing.

A major focus was what he, as a child, came to incorrectly believe about himself due to the neglect. He suffered from self-blame, which eroded his self-esteem and increased his sense of despair.

Over time, Ray was able to develop empathy and compassion for his mother's situation. She never had the benefit of treatment nor the resources, financial or emotional, to change her circumstances. Because of her lifestyle, she intentionally remained estranged from any extended family who could have assisted Ray. At one point in a session, Ray stated, "I think she was as lonely as I was."

As his empathy grew, he was able to release years of anger and bitterness. I helped him understand that forgiveness doesn't mean that you minimize an injustice or the events that occurred. In an act of forgiveness, you acknowledge the harm and release the toxic negative feelings that have consumed you.

I helped Ray understand that he would still feel times of sadness and disappointment when he thought about his childhood, but the rage and bitterness would be gone. The process would leave him more whole and connected.

After several sessions, Ray wanted to forgive his mother in a concrete way. I suggested he write her a letter, and he did. He went to the cemetery with his wife and read the letter at the grave site. He became very emotional and told her that he wanted "her soul to now be at peace," and that by forgiving her, she was helping him in his sobriety. Ray was able to find an authentic place to connect with his mother and finally feel less isolated and alone. I believe this process was crucial to Ray's ability to grow in his recovery. By reducing his anger and bitterness, he closed a door the negative committee frequently used to make him vulnerable.

I should point out that before Ray worked on these issues he had with his mother, he asked his wife and

9 - FORGIVENESS AND ACCEPTING CONSEQUENCES

son to forgive him for the years of difficulty his drinking created for the family. Ray had many genuine regrets. Working with his sponsor and with the support of therapy, he was able to make amends to his family. This initial process with his wife and son helped to introduce Ray to the powerful healing elements of forgiveness. He was humbled that his wife had stayed with him through so many arduous years, and that his son reconnected with him. The act of their forgiveness allowed Ray to experience firsthand the healing that occurs. After Ray forgave his mother, I encouraged him to focus on the future and the husband, father, and man he wanted to be. He was able to integrate his past and move from a childhood victim to an adult survivor. His bitterness gave way to powerful compassion and life purpose.

Remember that Ray and Lynn opened their home on holidays for newly recovering people who needed a safe and welcoming place to go? I suspect that Ray's dedication to this activity was fueled by his recollection that his mother never had that safe place to go, and neither did he.

Forgiveness was a very important element in Ray's long-term success with sobriety.

ESTELLA'S STORY CONTINUES...

I introduced Estella's story in Chapter 3. She left her marriage to an active alcoholic in another state and relocated to San Diego to support her own recovery. Estella was able to successfully navigate the first year of separation and a painful holiday season. The divorce was sadly very nasty, as Carl did not display any insight or empathy for her. He was caught in his disease and was spiteful and mean. Estella tried hard to let go of *expectations. Although married for over 20 years, she ended up with few resources or possessions because she decided not to prolong litigation. This was probably a wise move given the drama and high emotional intensity.*

Unfortunately, what bothered Estella the most was not the actual loss of possessions or resources, but rather what his demeaning behavior implied about her value. Her negative committee constantly assaulted her. Although Estella's core beliefs about herself were sound, she often found herself enraged over Carl's treatment of her. On a cognitive level, she understood he was actively alcoholic and incapable of the insight and self-reflection he would need to divorce in a healthy and supportive way. On the other hand, his treatment of her left her feeling emotionally abused and unable to make peace with the time they had together.

Estella came back into therapy to work on this issue after she and her ex-husband finalized the divorce. Estella comprehended that the toxic anger she was experiencing made her vulnerable to relapse. She also recognized that Carl's alcoholism was severe. At one point, he was found unconscious in his home and hospitalized, yet still rejected any treatment for his drinking. There would be no reconciliation of resentments between the two parties. Slowly, Estella understood that forgiveness of Carl would be the only effective antidote to her pain and suffering.

Estella had found a good deal of support at her church. At my urging, she spoke to the pastor about the notion of forgiveness. She brought these insights into her therapy. The act of forgiveness was meant to free her, to cleanse her toxic state of anger and restore her emotional equilibrium. She read about forgiveness and

9 - FORGIVENESS AND ACCEPTING CONSEQUENCES

decided to journal about it. Over the course of several weeks she devoted herself to writing. Estella found journaling to be a cathartic experience.

She completed her journal writing and sent Carl a short note. She told him she suffered from the same disease of alcoholism and understood its powerful effect on the mind and body. She told him that she forgave him for his poor behavior prior to her departure and during the divorce. She wished him health and happiness.

Interestingly, Estella noted that after she truly forgave Carl, she could look back at a happy time in their early marriage and not become enraged with bitterness that it didn't work out. Forgiveness helped her come to a place of acceptance. The early years of her marriage were wonderful and she was able to remember them that way. The last few years of the marriage were terrible, and she acknowledged that without having to connect with toxic anger and bitterness. She accepted that experience and forgave Carl for the role he played. Incidentally, Carl never acknowledged her note. It didn't matter. Estella said what she needed to say.

"Collective Wisdom" tells us that "FORGIVENESS IS AN IMPORTANT FACTOR IN HEALING." It is a powerful antidote to coercive and toxic emotions. It frees the spirit and fosters acceptance and sound judgment. It's a transformative ingredient essential to ongoing recovery.

FURTHER INFORMATION

JOURNALING

I want to take a moment and acknowledge "journaling" which is a powerful recovery tool. It's an important recovery activity that can reap many benefits. Not only will journaling help clarify feelings, it will also help the writer discover his or her authentic voice. A commitment to journaling will focus attention on self-exploration. It will help stimulate the ability to be honest and promote the gratitude that is so essential to lasting recovery.

Combining journaling with weekly therapy can prove invaluable. As feelings, experiences, and regrets come to the surface, they can be examined in a safe environment and understood in the context of growth and healing. Journaling can be particularly helpful to those impacted by substance abuse who are also adult children of alcoholics/addicts. Many individuals will be able to connect the dots with journaling and find their authentic voice free of the fears that plagued their childhoods.

I encourage clients not to worry about any particular format when they journal. Don't worry about spelling or punctuation. Those concerns can distract from connecting with your emotions and inner voice. The process of journaling can help you address perfectionism if that is an issue with which you struggle, as many individuals growing up in an alcoholic home do. Just begin with whatever is on your mind and go from there. Often clients will write about a here-and-now experience that leads them to a childhood recollection that they can explore. Journaling can often help relieve anger and grief, as it did for my client Estella. Journaling provides an opportunity to attend to your heart and soul. It can be thought of as an important element of self-care and a step in the direction of self-actualization. Journaling can

9 - FORGIVENESS AND ACCEPTING CONSEQUENCES

help you create a blueprint for your future. It can help you identify red flags, priorities, and values.

I would suggest ending each journal entry with an affirmation. Find affirmations that speak to you and repeat them regularly both verbally and in writing. They are an important antidote to the negative committee and a powerful form of intention. Affirmations embrace optimism, compassion, and confidence. These are vital ingredients to our health and wellbeing.

At first, the process of journaling may feel awkward and uncomfortable. If It is unfamiliar you will be in an Unknown Zone. Nevertheless, if you stay with it, the rewards will become apparent. Journaling creates great intimacy with oneself. Many individuals feel a connection with themselves that they have never experienced before in their adult lives. Please don't underestimate the enormous benefits journaling and affirmation can bring to your recovery.

REFERENCE LIST

[1] L.G. DiStefano, LCSW and M. Hohman, Ph.D., *The Paradigm Developmental Model of Treatment: A Clinical Guide for Counselors Working with Substance Abusers and the Chemically Dependent.* San Diego, CA: Montezuma Publishing, 2010.

[2] Alcoholics Anonymous World Services, Inc. (2016, Aug.). *The Twelve Steps of Alcoholics Anonymous* [Online]. Available: http://www.aa.org/assets/en_US/smf-121_en.pdf

[3] Greater Good Magazine. (2017). *What Is Forgiveness?* [Online]. Available: http://greatergood.berkeley.edu/topic/forgiveness/definition#what_is

[4] Nelson Mandela Foundation-Life and Times of Nelson Mandela. (2017) *Biography of Nelson Mandela* [Online]. Available: https://www.nelsonmandela.org/content/page/biography

[5] Nelson Mandela Centre of Memory. (2017). *Nelson Mandela: Prison Years* [Online]. Available: https://www.google.com/culturalinstitute/beta/exhibit/kwliugUhu8QclA

[6] Wikipedia. (2017, Oct. 20). *Nelson Mandela* [Online]. Available: https://en.wikipedia.org/w/index.php?title=Nelson_Mandela&oldid=806173861

[7] J. Blake. (2010, Jan. 14). *'Invictus' hero recalls day Mandela transformed South Africa* [Online]. Available: http://www.cnn.com/2009/SHOWBIZ/Movies/12/10/invictus/

[8] NobelPrize.org. (2014, Jan. 29). *The Nobel Peace Prize 1993* [Online]. Available: http://www.nobelprize.org/nobel_prizes/peace/laureates/1993/

[9] D. Gover. (2013, Dec. 6). *Nelson Mandela: Four Acts of Forgiveness That Showed South Africa Path Away from Apartheid* [Online]. Available: www.ibtimes.co.uk/nelson-mandela-forgiveness-south-africa-apartheid-528153

[10] J. Carlin, *Playing the Enemy: Nelson Mandela and The Game that Made a Nation.* New York, NY: Penguin Press, 2008.

[11] Wikipedia. (2017, Oct. 19). *Invictus* (film) [Online]. Available: https://en.wikipedia.org/w/index.php?title=Invictus_(film)&oldid=806101103

CHAPTER 10

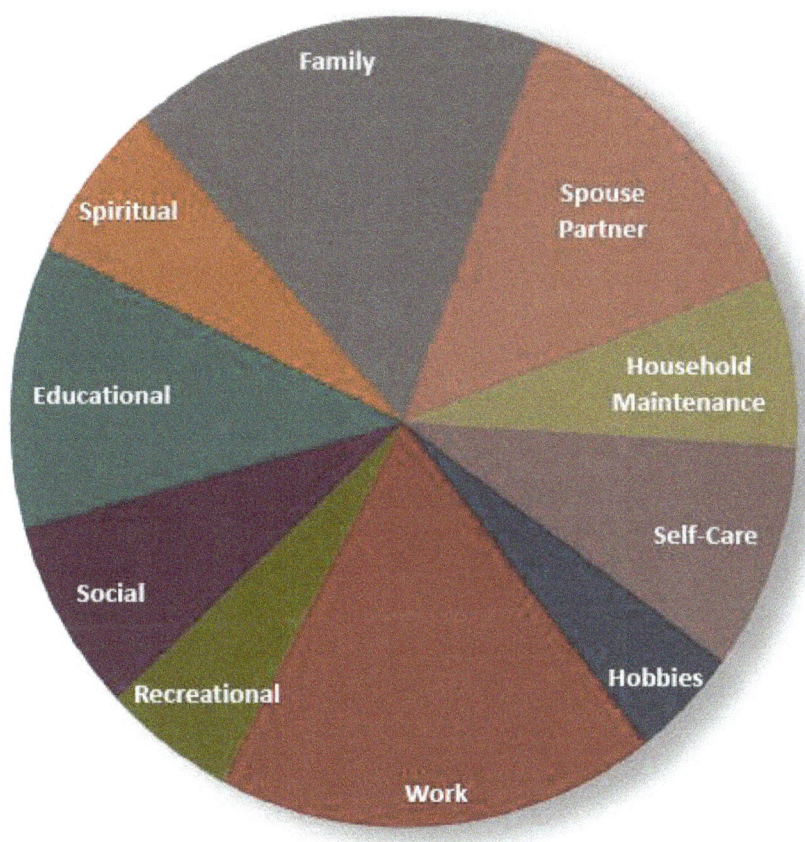

THEME 10
SELF-REGULATION

The 10th theme of the PDMT Model is Self-Regulation [1], and is perhaps the most important theme in ongoing recovery. At this point, an individual has completed initial treatment, counseling, etc., and hopefully will continue to monitor his or her long-term recovery. Many individuals continue with self-help meeting participation. Some individuals may not participate in or continue with self-help groups. Nevertheless, in either case, an individual must actively focus on self-regulation to keep the life balance and thought clarity that supports sobriety. The potential to relapse increases if a person loses the emotional balance and equilibrium inherent in recovery.

What is self-regulation? It is the action or process of healthy self-management and the integration of positive behavioral change. It's being conscious of our needs and stress levels and attending to our mental and physical health on a daily basis. In the PDMT Model, self-regulation is also the title of Paradigm 3 [1]. This Paradigm begins with Theme 9.

By the end of this stage of recovery, Paradigm 3, the individual has been exposed to a variety of tools and resources. They have learned about them self, identified areas of vulnerability (avoidance, anger, loneliness, etc.), and are following a plan of rituals, routines, and resources that supports their recovery. Also, by this stage, an individual should be actively involved in managing their specific red flags and relapse warning signs. Additionally, in Paradigm 3, clients are often involved in resolving family of origin issues, as they usually have the psychological resilience at this point to deal with painful childhood and family of origin issues [1].

10 - SELF-REGULATION

Self-regulation occurs in the here and now. On a daily basis, individuals in recovery attend to rigorous self-monitoring which creates balance and wholeness in their lives. Recovery continually reinforces resilience. It is an ongoing process of self-regulation.

THE THREE RS

Focusing on the following areas can be extremely helpful as individuals engage in self-regulation. The activities that constitute the Rituals, Routines, and Resources of Recovery should be based on an individual's specific issues and relapse dynamics. Focusing on the three Rs provides a strong foundation to build a stable sobriety.

RITUALS

Establishing specific rituals in recovery can help anchor an individual's self-regulation. For example, in the A.A. fellowship and other 12-step groups, individuals are given tokens (sobriety coins) to represent the amount of time the member has remained sober. Attending a meeting and receiving a token is a powerful way to acknowledge the progress a person has made.

People in other self-help programs often go to yearly conferences or retreats that are recovery-oriented. This ritual provides an opportunity to maintain friendships and focus on renewal and commitment. A similar ritual is a yearly camping trip with other individuals in recovery or a yearly motorcycle ride to the mountains. These types of rituals help keep us connected and renewed.

ROUTINES

Developing sobriety-based routines are essential to anchor ongoing recovery. Don't think, "I want to catch a self-help meeting this week." According to the collective wisdom of my clients, that type of commitment is too vague and easy to dismiss. Rather, pick a day and time to attend a meeting. Agreeing to pick someone up or meeting a person for coffee before the meeting also helps to keep the commitment solid.

Remember H.A.L.T. from Chapter 7? Establishing routines that support the management of H.A.L.T. are fundamental. A meal plan that includes regular mealtimes, vitamin supplements, and nutritious food is optimal. Following a sleep schedule with regular hours is essential [2]. Finding outlets to discuss your feelings and emotions can go a long way to staying positive, and connection with others is an antidote for loneliness.

Over the years the "Collective Wisdom" has been unequivocal that "THERE IS FREEDOM IN ROUTINES." The more positive behaviors that are established as routines, the less likely an individual will be to debate with themselves whether or not to do something. A morning run, daily meditation, a set dinner hour, a nightly call to a support person, attending a weekly faith-based service, and a regular set of self-help meetings all contribute to the anchoring of recovery.

I also outlined the S.E.T. the Day Routine in Chapter 7. This routine can be a powerful recovery tool if practiced on a daily basis. In the book, *Freedom from Addiction*, David Simon, M.D. and Deepak Chopra, M.D., discuss a comparable method of self-review they call "recapitulation." They state, "taking time to review our actions and noticing when we responded from fear rather than wisdom enables us to learn from our past..." They also assert, "performing this process on a daily basis prevents the accumulation of unsettled issues [3:p.28-29]."

RESOURCES

The third R represents the ongoing and changing resources that help stabilize and facilitate recovery. Initially, a person may rely on counseling or a treatment program as they begin sobriety. You may follow this with financial counseling or marital therapy. As a person grows and life changes occur, utilizing appropriate resources is fundamental to continued stabilization.

Let me say this another way. The negative committee is constantly on the lookout for opportunities to make drug or alcohol use the best option. Why speak to a counselor about debt when a drink can make it all go away? It sounds crazy, but trust me, I have heard versions of that remark for years.

Truth be told, nothing works as fast as a drink or other drug for immediate relief. That's why resources need to be front and center in recovery. A person may need to wait for an appointment or consultation, but if their mind has become accustomed to thinking in terms of being proactive with resources, they can often avoid the "poor me's" that can end in picking up that drink or drug.

The Three Rs and the management of H.A.L.T. are vital components to building a strong and stable recovery.

THE GROWTH ZONE

It should be noted that by the end of Paradigm 3, clients have experienced several years of quality sobriety. This becomes the time for individuals to move out of their comfort zones and engage in growth-oriented activities. Individuals often confuse the normal fear and trepidation that accompanies movement out of a comfort zone with a relapse dynamic. Therapy is often useful in helping individuals differentiate between normal anxiety and discomfort, as well as the uneasy feelings that often precede a relapse. Moving through the Unknown Zone of change is an important theme of this paradigm [1:p.155].

THE BALANCE WHEEL

Another aspect of self-regulation is captured in the balance wheel (see diagram on page 197). Everyone's life is different. Some people have marriages, children, pets, or educational commitments. Other people have intense career or vocational pursuits. Therefore, each person's balance wheel will be somewhat different. What is important is the concept of equilibrium.

For many years I provided wellness seminars to the employees of a large local institution. When I would teach the work/life balance class, I would ask participants to draw on their wheel what currently exists and what they would like to exist. Many people would initially split the wheel in two with sleep/eat on one half of the wheel and work on the other. It was a sad commentary. Over time, many of the individuals I worked with strove to improve their balance and create a more sustainable wheel.

One of the takeaways from this work was a critical stress management realization. When stress goes up, what a person should do to manage the stress should also go up. Unfortunately, the exact opposite frequently occurs.

When stress goes up, the things we do to manage the stress actually go down. We think, "things are crazy busy, I don't have time to exercise, or eat a meal, or call a friend, or do something relaxing." Instead of providing ourselves with relief and respite, we further aggravate the situation by not bringing our stress levels down. Stress management is not rocket science. However, many people make the fundamental mistake of reducing their stress management options during intense periods of stress rather than increasing them. It may feel counter-intuitive, but a successful stress management response is to meet the level of stress with activities and strategies of sufficient portion [4:p.371].

CO-OCCURRING DISORDERS

An area of particular importance concerns those individuals diagnosed with co-occurring disorders. These individuals require recovery planning and self-management for both their alcohol/drug problem and their mental health condition. For example, if an individual with an alcohol problem also suffers from depression, they will need resources and plans in place to address the depression, as well as the alcohol use disorder. This might include:

- Being under the care of a psychiatrist.
- Taking antidepressant medication as prescribed.
- Working with an individual therapist.
- Keeping a mood chart to track feeling states on a daily basis.

- Focusing on little victories by adjusting expectations of self.
- Identifying relapse triggers on both sides of the street.
- Understanding the inter-relationship between both conditions.

Resources for managing a substance use disorder and a mental health condition are essential to long-term sobriety.

FLEXIBLE THINKING, MANAGED EMOTIONS, MODERATE BEHAVIOR

I co-authored a book and a coaching manual, *New Ways for Work,* with my friend and colleague, Bill Eddy, LCSW, Esq. We wrote this manual to help individuals who often experience conflict and have difficulty in the workplace. In this manual, we present a cognitive-behavioral method designed to help individuals reduce their conflict and improve their self-regulation. We focus on four skill areas of self-regulation that are also exceptionally useful and appropriate for individuals to work on in early recovery [5].

FLEXIBLE THINKING

One of the biggest barriers to successful problem solving is all-or-nothing thinking. Individuals with all-or-nothing thinking tend to view situations in the extremes. Things are either wonderful and terrific or horrible and a disaster. There are no "gray areas," only black or white. This type of thinking impairs effective problem-solving. Such extremes in thinking lead to heightened and often upset emotions [5:p.19].

10 - SELF-REGULATION

Some examples of all or nothing thinking are:
- It's my way or the highway!
- Everyone is against me. There's nothing I can do!
- I've got this down, I don't need anyone's input!

Some examples of flexible thinking are:
- There's more than one solution to this problem.
- Let me understand where they are coming from so we can work this out.
- What are my options here? [5:p.19]

MANAGED EMOTIONS

Being unable to manage our negative emotions can distract us from achieving our goals and often will create new and worse problems for us. Learning to manage our emotions can make a big difference in being able to remain clean and sober. If emotions escalate, it often leads to extreme behaviors that frequently are regrettable. Individuals can spend a lot of time trying to fix the damages caused by extreme emotions [5:p.19]. Some examples of extreme or unmanaged emotions are:
- Refusing to cooperate out of anger.
- Creating tension by giving a person the silent treatment.
- Yelling at someone because you took what they said the wrong way.

Some examples of managed emotions are:
- Expressing disappointment in a calm, non-threatening manner.

- Talking feelings over after a period of reflection and thought.
- Stating, "I need a break for a few minutes," and getting some air [5:p.19].

Later in this chapter I will discuss E.A.R. Techniques, which are a very helpful tool in managing emotions and de-escalating conflict.

MODERATE BEHAVIOR

A person can manage their emotions more easily once thinking becomes flexible. This helps create behavior that is moderate and not extreme. Moderate behavior can lead to collaboration, compromise, and other positive outcomes. Extreme behavior frequently results in heightened conflict, name-calling, bullying, regrettable decision-making and, frequently, relapse [5:p.19].

Some examples of extreme behavior are:
- Storming out of a room in anger.
- Physically pushing someone.
- Walking out on a job.

Some examples of moderate behavior are:
- Speaking in a clear non-aggressive tone of voice.
- Making gestures or overtures of cooperation.
- Responding in a manner that demonstrates empathy, attention, and respect [5:p.19].

CHECKING YOURSELF

We developed this last piece of the *New Ways* method to encourage individuals to reflect on their behavior and recognize where they have been successful and what needs to be improved. This is a valuable tool for self-regulation. Working with a counselor or therapist on self-regulation tools provides an opportunity to reflect on and expose patterns that can be damaging. It also provides an opportunity to reinforce positive changes in thinking, emotions, and behavior [5:p.19].

BRIAN'S STORY CONTINUES....

I introduced Brian in Chapter 2. Brian went into a treatment program after hitting his personal bottom. He followed recommendations and gave up his apartment and moved to a sober living residence. He went back to school and became an Alcohol and Drug Counselor, and he engaged in weekly therapy for several years. He also managed his depression with medication, psychiatric oversight, and rigorous attention to self-regulation.

Brian also recognized the value of scheduling recovery-oriented activities as routines in his life. He attended specific weekly meetings, developed a meaningful relationship with a sponsor, and completed his certification requirements. With a great deal of thought and consideration, he moved out of the sober living residence after more than two years and obtained his own apartment. Slowly he created a functional and comfortable space for himself.

During his college internship, Brian worked at a prestigious treatment program that quickly recognized his counseling talents and keen intellect. Upon graduation, the program offered him an entry-level position. So, a few months past his third sobriety anniversary, he had both a good job and his own apartment.

Brian was acutely aware of his personal relapse warning signs. Isolation was a major issue he needed to monitor continually. He struggled for years with depression and although it was now managed with medication, his tendency to keep to himself was part of his comfort zone and natural reflexes. So he challenged himself and met friends at the facility where he worked. Brian arranged hikes and other outings with colleagues who quickly became friends. He created a support system that was instrumental to his self-regulation process.

Eventually, his friends encouraged him to start to date. He had several girlfriends over the years but none during the time he was clean and sober. Dating was a scary process for him, but he understood the importance of connection and the value of intimacy in his life. His friends helped him sign up for a dating site and he began to meet women for coffee and meals.

He was forthright about the fact that he was in recovery and only dated individuals that were comfortable with the fact that he was not interested in going to clubs or bars. He did not require that a person also be in recovery, but was honest with the fact that he wasn't interested in kissing someone who smelled of booze and needed alcohol to socialize and have a good time. These facts limited his prospects somewhat, but his handsome good looks and warm nature were very attractive.

One day he came to a session and announced that he thought he had met "the one!". Although she was eight years his junior, she was bright and articulate, insightful, and extremely supportive. She had just become licensed as a cosmetician and was fortunate to have found work in a prestigious salon. To be honest, there were no red flags that he, his family, or I could identify. Brian felt she was somewhat immature due to her younger age, but nothing serious. Frankly, an older woman would be more likely to want to settle down and start a family, and I didn't believe Brian was emotionally ready for that. The age difference gave them both the opportunity to be a couple without the pressure and expectations associated with an older partner.

They had apartments near one another. She had a roommate and his place was extremely small. Nevertheless, they dated for a year utilizing both spaces as best they could. They worked on and resolved a host of issues regarding accommodating his recovery and her job demands during that first year.

I was impressed with the depth of Brian's emotional growth, his commitment to the relationship, and his continued focus on his recovery. He announced in session one day that they had decided to rent a new place together once his lease had expired. It would be close to their one-year anniversary. I could see no downside to the plan. Brian was ready to complete weekly therapy. He understood that he could resume whenever he needed to.

Several months later Brian called for an appointment. He was anxious and distraught. The couple had recently found and furnished a lovely two-bedroom apartment. According to Brian, they had worked well putting it together and he thought his girlfriend Nancy was happy. Unfortunately, she was not. The move created a good deal of conflict for her. She went into therapy and apparently recognized that moving in together created a commitment she was not yet ready to make. She told Brian she loved him but felt that she didn't want to make a decision now on the person with whom she would choose to spend the rest of her life. She joined him for a session with me at the urging of her therapist and finally told him she felt compelled to explore other relationships before deciding on a marriage partner.

Brian was devastated. All the self-regulation tools, the support system, and his program went into high gear and helped him to not drink. The "Collective Wisdom" my clients shared is that, "YOUR RECOVERY PROGRAM HAS TO WORK ON YOUR WORST DAY, NOT JUST YOUR BEST." This is eminently true.

It was a very arduous time for Brian. They dismantled their apartment. Nancy went back to her parents' home to regroup. Fortunately, Brian found a smaller studio in the same complex, which was a tremendous financial help. The management company was excellent and worked with him to exchange units. He handled the initial stages of the breakup as well as could be expected. The latter stages were more difficult. He was plagued with self-doubt. He felt he was a failure as a boyfriend. He appreciated that Nancy was honest with him and believed she told him as soon as she had figured out her feelings. However, there were days of anger and intense rage. During that dismal year, Brian utilized every recovery and self-regulation tool he had learned to maintain his sobriety. He frequently tried to isolate (his old M.O.) but his friends were assertive. He maintained his meeting schedule and contact with his sponsor. He resumed weekly therapy and I saw first-hand the emotional pain he was managing on a daily basis. It took a long time for Brian to heal.

One of the discussions we had that I believe impacted his perspective, concerned the "gifts" this experience had provided. Obviously, no one wants to

10 - SELF-REGULATION

endure the pain and upheaval that a breakup creates. But I pointed out to Brian that the experience provided us with very valuable pieces of information, so valuable they could be considered "gifts."

Brian looked incredulous and said, "You're not serious; are you kidding me?"

"Not at all," I responded.

"You must be joking?" he said.

How could such an awful situation be valuable? I explained as Brian listened intently.

Before Brian had become involved with Nancy, we didn't know what his capacity for consistent intimacy would be. We didn't know if he could maintain the responsibilities inherent in a couple's relationship on a daily basis. We didn't know how he would handle true adversity and pain. We also didn't know if his recovery could hold up under prolonged adverse circumstances. But now, thanks to the relationship with Nancy, we knew. Brian had navigated a very difficult time period using all the tools at his disposal. He didn't walk away from his program: he embraced it. Brian learned much about himself and his resilience through this experience. Eventually, he came to appreciate the "gifts" that this experience had given him.

He now recognizes that he is capable of a long-term, committed relationship. He can now picture himself as a husband and father and is looking forward to those life passages. Today, Brian is dating a woman closer to his age and he is very positive about the future of their relationship. The self-regulation tools he utilizes daily continue to provide immeasurable benefits to his life.

UTILIZING E.A.R. TECHNIQUES

In addition to the previously mentioned manual, I co-authored the book, *It's All Your Fault at Work: Managing Narcissists and Other High Conflict People,* with Bill Eddy, LCSW, Esq. in 2015 [6]. We were thrilled when we learned the book won a prestigious award the same year from Axiom Business Book Awards, recognized in the area of Human Resources and Employee Training.

Employees across the country are in need of skills to help manage communication in increasingly difficult work environments. We recently learned that a publisher in China bought the rights to publish and distribute *It's All Your Fault at Work* in that country. Obviously, the need to develop greater skills for interacting with others in the workplace is not just a phenomenon occurring in America.

This book teaches techniques to help individuals manage high-conflict personalities in both their personal and work environments. The techniques we teach are aimed at de-escalating conflict by helping to calm the high-conflict individual by moving them from defensive right-brain responses to problem-solving left-brain responses. Individuals are generally reactive and aggressive when they are stuck in defensive right brain thinking, but become more flexible in their thinking and responses once they are operating from their problem-solving left brain [6]. This knowledge motivated Bill Eddy to conceptualize the E.A.R. techniques in his first book, *It's All Your Fault!: 12 Tips For Managing People Who Blame Others For Everything* [7:p.221].

E.A.R. stands for Empathy, Attention, and Respect. It's a simple technique but requires an individual, in the face of an escalating situation with another person, to respond with E.A.R. Statements. These statements, delivered with sincerity, can calm a situation and move an individual into a more reasonable set of responses.

I am addressing this topic because I have found in my clinical work that clients in recovery who utilize E.A.R. Responses in their daily interactions find themselves calmer and less likely to inadvertently escalate any conflict.

Simply put, this approach is a valuable tool for individuals in recovery and an effective method of communication with anyone. By demonstrating Empathy for the other person, you are seeing a situation from their perspective and appreciating the problems or issues associated with their situation. By demonstrating Attention, you are giving the person your full concentration, which will help to increase your thorough comprehension of the issue. By demonstrating Respect for the other person, you are supporting their self-esteem, acknowledging their value, and facilitating a positive connection with them.

An important element of E.A.R. is that you do not have to agree with the content. However, by responding with empathy, attention, and respect, situations frequently de-escalate. Perhaps more importantly to those in recovery, it provides a standard of communication designed to keep emotions managed and behavior appropriate. E.A.R. can be adopted as a Recovery Routine (from the three Rs) in that it becomes our go-to process in response to others. It's also an easy technique to remember when emotions begin to escalate [6][7].

FURTHER INFORMATION

A BODY-CENTERED APPROACH TO RECOVERY

The vast majority of treatment approaches are some variation of talk therapy, either in group settings or individual sessions. Today however, there are a number of approaches that initiate change and healing through the body.

I recently spoke with Soleil Hepner, C-IAYT, a certified Yoga Therapist in private practice in San Diego specializing in trauma, pain, and recovery. She is also the Program Director for Phoenix Rising Yoga Therapy, an accredited program that merges yoga practice with psychotherapy. I asked her to elaborate on a body-centered approach to recovery. She responded, "A body-centered approach can be advantageous because it's common that someone who has experienced significant trauma in the past [abuse, neglect, addictive parents] cannot access the memory and emotional reaction through verbal means, yet these traumas may be the very source of the addictive pattern." She further stated, "A growing body of scientific research on the brain reveals that the self-regulation mechanisms that we rely on can be shut down on a neurological level in the aftermath of significant traumas. This is most evident when you just don't have the words to describe your experience. You are stuck or in relapse. In such cases, a body-focused approach may liberate the individual and allow for significant recovery."

Current body approaches that work on the neurological level might include Eye Movement Desensitization and Reprocessing (EMDR), Embodied Mindfulness, and Phoenix Rising Yoga Therapy (PRYT).

10 - SELF-REGULATION

I asked Ms. Hepner if she could provide a case example from her clinical experience.

"An example is JD who was self-medicating with alcohol after the traumatizing loss of her child," Ms. Hepner replied. "In her regular 12-step group sessions, JD felt numb and distant from emotion with little to say. In her PRYT sessions, she noticed her body shaking, her breath shallow, and she wanted to flee. Being supported by the practitioner to compassionately witness her body's sensations, JD eventually found the words to connect to deep sadness and pain, learning to tolerate her great loss without needing the alcohol to cover."

In the course of our discussion, Ms. Hepner went on to describe the process.

"In a series of one-hour sessions, a PRYT therapist facilitates an increased awareness of present-moment body sensations that are neurologically linked to past traumas. Practicing a non-judgmental attitude while observing these sensations allows a person to explore these past traumas and increase their brain's resilience to the relapse triggers, which may have inhibited their recovery."

For more on the neuroscience behind these approaches Ms. Hepner, recommends the book, *The Body Keeps the Score: Brain, Mind, and Body in the Healing of Trauma*, by Bessel van der Kolk M.D. [8]

There are some individuals with specific traumas that would not be appropriate for a body-centered approach. I recommend you discuss this issue with your therapist or current health care provider and be sure to verify the credentials and accreditations of the provider and or program in which you are interested.

TAPPING

Jack Canfield and Dave Andrews, in their comprehensive 2016 book, *The 30 Day Sobriety Solution: How to Cut Back or Quit Drinking in the Privacy of Your Own Home,* discuss the concept of tapping [9:p.212]. This technique is commonly known as EFT - Emotional Freedom Techniques or Tapping. The authors explain that "First developed as the five-minute phobia cure by Dr. Roger Callahan to cure phobias, fears, and anxieties, it was later further developed and popularized by Gary Craig, Dawson Church, Nick Ortner, and others to relieve stress, release negative emotions, make physical symptoms (including pain) disappear, dissolve, and replace limiting beliefs, and reduce or eliminate cravings and addictions."

This technique involves focused thought with finger tapping on a series of seven to twelve acupuncture points. Individuals can perform the technique on themselves, and according to the authors it can radically accelerate the process of recovery [9:p.213]. I suggest this book to anyone wanting to achieve sobriety and engage in recovery. It provides a wealth of resources both conventional and more cutting edge. The 30-Day Sobriety Solution is a comprehensive program that has an interactive website. I believe that many of the activities and resources discussed in *The 30-Day Sobriety Solution* are compatible with the PDMT Model and together provide individuals with a powerful set of tools to explore their relationship with alcohol and other drugs.

REFERENCE LIST

[1] L.G. DiStefano, LCSW and M. Hohman, Ph.D., *The Paradigm Developmental Model of Treatment: A Clinical Guide for Counselors Working with Substance Abusers and the Chemically Dependent.* San Diego, CA: Montezuma Publishing, 2010.

[2] Dr. John. (1971, Feb.). *The Essence of AA - H.A.L.T.* [Online]. Available: http://sobertransitions.org/Halt.html

[3] D. Simon, M.D. and D. Chopra, *Freedom from Addiction: The Chopra Center Method for Overcoming Destructive Habits.* Deerfield Beach, FL: Health Communications Inc., 2007, pp. 28-29.

[4] L.G. DiStefano, LCSW, *The Paradigm Developmental Model of Treatment Group Topics.* San Diego, CA: Montezuma Publishing, 2012, p. 371.

[5] B. Eddy, LCSW, Esq. and L.G. Distefano, LCSW, *New Ways for Work: Personal Skills for Productive Relationships—Coaching Manual.* Scottsdale, AZ: High Conflict Institute Press, 2015.

[6] B. Eddy, LCSW, Esq. and L.G. Distefano, LCSW, *It's All Your Fault at Work: Managing Narcissists and Other High Conflict People.* Scottsdale, AZ: Unhooked Books/High Conflict Institute Press, 2015.

[7] B. Eddy, LCSW, Esq., *It's All Your Fault!: 12 Tips for Managing People Who Blame Others for Everything.* Scottsdale, AZ: Janis Publications USA Inc., 2008, p. 221.

[8] B. van der Kolk M.D., *The Body Keeps the Score: Brain, Mind and Body in the Healing of Trauma.* New York, NY: Penguin Publishing Group, 2014.

[9] J. Canfield, and D. Andrews, *The 30 Day Sobriety Solution: How to Cut Back or Quit Drinking in the Privacy of Your Own Home.* New York, NY: Atria Books/Simon and Schuster, Inc., 2016, pp. 212, 213.

CHAPTER 11

THEME 11
MINDFULNESS

Mindfulness provides a useful cognitive alternative to A.A.'s 11th step: "Sought through prayer and meditation to improve our conscious contact with God, as we understood Him, praying only for knowledge of His will for us and the power to carry that out [1]."

Individuals who practice daily mindfulness live a life more balanced and enriched with gratitude. The dictionary defines mindfulness as "the practice of maintaining a nonjudgmental state of heightened or complete awareness of one's thoughts, emotions, or experiences on a moment-to-moment basis [2]."

I particularly like the definition of mindfulness used by Ronald D. Siegel, PsyD. In his book, *The Mindfulness Solution: Everyday Practices For Everyday Problems.,* he states mindfulness is "awareness of present experience with acceptance [3:p.27]."

As I discuss in my *Group Topics* book, it takes practice to live in the here and now and foster mindful observance, appreciation, and acceptance. Concentration and engagement of the senses bring a heightened awareness [4].

Alcoholics and addicts use chemicals to alter their mood and change their feeling state. Mindfulness is one of the methods a recovering person can practice that will help alter mood and positively change feelings. Mindful living contributes to a deep sense of gratitude for a wide variety of things. Living mindfully helps keep emotional connections working. The heightened awareness created by mindful living replenishes the human spirit. Although an individual's daily routine may not differ significantly, mindfully managing that routine can create great benefit for the individual. This implies taking the moments necessary to be fully aware and to engage our senses.

Simple tasks like driving to work, kissing your child, or sipping a cup of coffee can contribute to one's sense of wellbeing if fully experienced [4:p.394-396].

According to author Rebecca Crane, "mindfulness encourages individuals to process experience without judgment as it arises. This helps to change an individual's relationship with challenging thoughts and feelings [5:p. xviii]." Mindfulness techniques have been proven to enhance stress reduction and promote deep relaxation [5].

A morning meditation can allow a person to center himself or herself. Quiet time can serve the same function if it permits an individual time to self-reflect and experience an appreciation for the abundance that life has provided.

"Collective Wisdom" tells us that "RELAPSE LIVES IN A WORLD OF FEAR, UNHAPPINESS, AND EMOTIONAL DISCONNECTION." These seeds of relapse cannot grow easily in an environment strong in appreciation, positive regard, joy, and connection. Mindfulness helps determine positive choices that guide an individual's life. It stimulates value-centered decisions and helps to reinforce intuition. I think of mindfulness as a mental filter that trains our mind to focus on what is positive and life-enriching.

Individuals will vary in their understanding and reactions to this theme. Those that now engage in yoga or meditation as part of their new lifestyle might readily appreciate the value and benefits of mindful practices. Some people connect this theme with religious beliefs or spirituality and are put off by this association. The point of this theme is to live with appreciation in the moment. If your personal appreciation of the moment connects you to your spirituality, then that is an important association for you. Nevertheless, appreciation of the moment can also connect you to beauty, joy, serenity, and any number of positive feelings that feed the spirit and nurture the soul. The interpretation is what is important and meaningful to each person.

When we practice mindfulness, we recognize that the past is gone. That is not to say that we don't reflect on our behavior, enjoy memories, or make amends where appropriate. But we understand that life occurs fully in the moment. Also, we should take the time to think about and prepare ourselves for the future. However, until the future arrives, we won't know all the variables or conditions and therefore can only speculate on what might be the best course of action. The moment provides the best opportunity to deeply connect with life and savor with all our senses the vast wonder it holds.

CLASSIC MINDFULNESS MEDITATION TECHNIQUES

According to noted author Elizabeth Scott, any activity that you perform where you stay fully present can count as a mindfulness meditation technique, and when practiced regularly can enhance your life [6]. Several of the techniques discussed by Scott are:

> SOUNDS - Focus mindfully on the sounds in your environment; this can calm the mind and create connection [6].
> SENSATIONS - Pay focused attention to sensations you feel in your body; this can provide a useful meditative experience [6].
> BREATHING - Many people utilize the art of breathing as an effective mindfulness technique.

11 - MINDFULNESS

> Concentration on breathing can lead to physical and emotional relaxation [6].
> TASTE - Mindful eating can create a heightened sense of taste, providing pleasure and a sense of wellbeing [6].

Sight can also focus mindfulness. To intensely observe nature and elements of the environment can create a strong sense of connection with our surroundings and enhance our awareness.

Let's consider a scenario to identify opportunities for mindfulness in the course of a typical day.

A DAY IN THE LIFE OF PETER

Peter is an executive of a mid-size biotech company, and has worked at this firm for eight years. He is re-married with two grown children.

Peter wakes before the alarm. He puts on his workout clothes and drives the short distance to the beach. It's a beautiful drive lined with flowering and colorful foliage, but Peter's mind is on an upcoming work presentation he must make in several days. He locks the car and begins his daily three-mile brisk walk. The ocean is gleaming, and the seagulls are hunting their breakfast as Peter fumbles with his headset. He spends the duration of the walk leaving phone messages and instructions to various employees. He rushes home for a quick shower and gulps down a cup of coffee and breakfast bar as he heads out the door. As he is about to leave, his wife Jean calls out, "Hey, bye, have a nice day!" He turns and walks over to her giving her a peck on the lips, "You too, and please remember to pick up the dry cleaning."

It is another beautiful ride to the office as Peter listens to messages. He arrives and walks to his office. Several people greet him with "Good morning." He mumbles "you too," but does not stop until he reaches his desk. He is reading a memo when his secretary arrives with another cup of coffee. He nods his appreciation but doesn't make eye contact.

His first meeting of the morning is with a department head who is concerned about the performance of a key employee. Peter is courteous but distracted, thinking about the new building project he will make a presentation on later in the week. He tells the manager to handle it and keep him posted, but asks no questions, nor does he offer any ideas or perspective.

Peter works through lunch, eating a sandwich that was delivered from the deli down the block. Outdoors it's a crisp sunny day, but Peter decides he needs to work and remains in his office. His eldest daughter Maria calls as he is finishing his lunch. She wants to confirm plans for him and Jean to attend a weekend event for his six-year-old granddaughter. Maria relates a humorous incident regarding the kids, but Peter doesn't absorb the story as he already has re-engaged with his e-mails.

Later in the day, his wife Jean calls to check on dinner plans. She pleasantly offers to wait for him so that they could have dinner together. However, he responds that it would be better for her to eat sooner and to leave him a dish; he wants to tie-up some loose ends.

He returns home at about 8:00 pm. He gives his wife another peck on the lips, undresses, and proclaims he is starved. Jean wants to tell him about her day, but remains quiet as she knows he wants to eat. Peter finds

11 - MINDFULNESS

the plate, does a quick heat-up in the microwave and eats his dinner standing at the counter.

This story, for the purposes of illustration, is full of missed opportunities to be mindful. It captures many situations that people regularly experience. Let's identify those situations and what a more mindful approach could have created.

REVIEW OF MISSED OPPORTUNITIES FOR MINDFULNESS

#1) He misses viewing the beautiful foliage on the way to the beach.
Taking a few moments and being mindful of the scenery would have started his day with a boost of serenity and calm.

#2) He misses really looking at the ocean and watching the seagulls.
Taking a few moments and being mindful of this scene could have sparked feelings of gratitude and good fortune.

#3) He takes a quick shower and misses an opportunity to mentally pause and enjoy the sensation of water warming his body.
Taking a few moments and being mindful of the sensations could have felt very restorative and relaxing.

#4) He gulps down coffee and quickly eats a breakfast bar.
Taking a few mindful moments to savor the coffee and enjoy the taste of the breakfast bar could have created a sense of satisfaction and contentment.

#5) He gives his wife a peck on the lips and reminds her of a chore.
Taking a few mindful moments to kiss his wife deeply and give her a hug before he reminded her of a chore could have greatly enhanced the connection and intimacy between the two of them.

#6) The ride to the office presents another missed opportunity to connect with nature.
A few mindful moments could have increased his sense of wellbeing.

#7) Peter arrives at the office and perfunctorily says good morning, not stopping to talk with anyone.
Taking a few mindful minutes to truly connect with a fellow employee could have created a closer bond and connection.

#8) Peter accepts coffee from his secretary but doesn't engage.
Taking a few mindful moments together could have increased the goodwill and started the day off with positive energy.

#9) Peter is courteous but disengaged with the department head.
Had Peter given this department head his full attention by being mindful in the moment, he could have greatly fostered a sense of unity and support that increases feelings of empowerment and empathy.

#10) Peter worked through lunch and missed an opportunity for a short walk (additional exercise) and the chance to connect with

11 - MINDFULNESS

others outside of work related issues. *Had Peter taken a short break and enjoyed a meal outside, the mindfulness of focusing on that meal could have provided an emotional respite that would have recharged his spirits for the rest of the day. Connecting with others outside of work issues strengthens relationships and creates goodwill.*

#11) Peter's daughter called and he's distracted when she tells him a humorous story. *Had Peter been mindful and concentrated on the conversation at hand he would have had an opportunity to feel joy and the emotional release that comes with a good laugh.*

#12) His wife offers to have dinner with him but he declines and continues to work. *Had Peter left the office and had dinner with his wife, and truly focused in a mindful way on their here-and-now interaction, he could have experienced deep connection, intimacy, and the wellbeing that comes from giving and receiving love.*

#13) Finally, Peter ends his day by eating standing up, rushing his food intake because he is so hungry. *Had Peter had his meal earlier with his wife, he would have added the enjoyment of food (tasting) to the other mindful benefits noted above.*

The reality of everyday life is full of opportunities to take a pause and utilize mindfulness to create an attitude adjustment or enhance a feeling state. Most people dream of resting and relaxing on a tropical island, but the truth is most of us don't have that opportunity on a regular basis. If we wait for a vacation to de-stress, the negative impact of anxiety, disconnection, and fear can seriously jeopardize sobriety.

Mindfulness can be done throughout the day. We can teach ourselves how to recharge our positive emotions and increase our gratitude. We can change our moods and alter our perception of reality by focusing deeply on here-and-now moments and cultivating the positive in our lives.

PRACTICE GRATITUDE

The dictionary defines gratitude as "the quality of being thankful; readiness to show appreciation for and to return kindness [7]."

Being grateful doesn't mean we ignore problems. However, living with gratitude is a key factor in maintaining a positive emotional equilibrium. Remember, the negative committee focuses on negative thoughts and interprets everyday situations in the most unaffirmative, unfavorable, and detrimental of ways.

Gratitude is a powerful antidote to negativity. When we "practice" gratitude along with mindfulness, we develop our cognitive abilities to reflect on a situation or event and extract something of worth. These tools may not solve the problem or necessarily avoid any unpleasantness associated with it. Nevertheless, they do help to keep our perspective, which will provide the mental conditions necessary for effective problem-

11 - MINDFULNESS

solving. Gratitude reminds us of the blessings, good fortune, and advantages we do have. Mindfulness helps to anchor our emotional equilibrium and build our resilience.

Anger and resentment significantly impact our ability to practice gratitude. Forgiveness, discussed in Chapter 9, is an important component in allowing the practice of gratitude to grow.

DEBORAH'S STORY CONTINUES...

Recall the physician, Deborah, I introduced in Chapter 1. She had a rigorous treatment plan outlined by the State Licensing Board's requirements. Today, Deborah credits the intense need for accountability as a factor in her success. Nevertheless, that does not negate the struggle Deborah experienced remaining positive and hopeful over the course of initial treatment. She candidly admitted to me, on more than one occasion, that she frequently wanted to walk away from the diversion program. It was, and admittedly should have been, an arduous ordeal. Deborah was emotionally honest and clear-headed enough to recognize that if she walked away from the program, she would within a matter of time, resume her drug use. She needed to stay the course and complete requirements.

In our treatment sessions, it became evident to Deborah that the one big area of control she did have involved her thoughts and the interpretations of what was happening to her. She understood the power of the negative committee and recognized that she couldn't assume she would naturally have the defenses necessary to withstand an assault. She had spent years cleverly hiding her addiction and sadly acknowledged that she was a master of deceit when it came to covering up her addictive behavior.

To quell the constant negative thoughts she was experiencing, she discerned that she needed a stronger self-motivating belief to anchor the behavioral requirements she was mandated to accomplish. In other words, she was doing behaviors, but she needed a more meaningful reason why.

She took solace in the famous 1946 book, Man's Search For Meaning, by highly acclaimed author Viktor Frankl. This book chronicled his experiences as an Auschwitz Concentration Camp inmate during World War II. To survive, Frankl described a method which involved identifying a purpose in life to feel positively about and then focusing on that outcome. According to Frankl, the way a prisoner imagined the future affected his longevity. At the core of Frankl's theory is the belief that man's primary motivational force is his search for meaning [8].

Odd as it may seem, Deborah's journey to discover meaning in her life was propelled by her desire to remain clean and sober. A surprising decision she made over time was that while she wanted to keep and clear her medical license, she no longer wanted to maintain a surgical practice. The nature of her practice was such that she frequently was disturbed at all hours of the night for emergency procedures. She had endured the schedule but came to believe that it posed a considerable threat to her sobriety. She felt that lifestyle was not conducive to her long-term recovery.

Her journey had interested her in addiction recovery and wellness issues. She could see herself consulting with treatment programs on the development of their chemical dependency programs. This new view of herself changed her perception of the arduous state requirements with which she dealt. She no longer was enduring the state requirements in order to resume her medical practice; instead, she was fulfilling those requirements to strengthen her recovery and to learn first-hand what was truly helpful to physicians in recovery.

An integral part of challenging her negative thoughts and finding meaning from her experience was her focus on gratitude. She decided to journal her gratitude and life experiences on a daily basis. She found that it helped her to truly acknowledge her good fortune and the blessings in her life.

GRATITUDE - AFFIRMATION - JOURNALING

"Collective Wisdom" tells us that "MINDFULNESS, GRATITUDE, JOURNALING, AND DAILY AFFIRMATIONS ARE A POWERFUL REMEDY TO NEGATIVITY." I elaborated on journaling in the "Further Information" section in Chapter 9.

An affirmation is an expression of gratitude. It's an empowering process that builds on our strengths and optimism. Noted author Melody Beattie may have said it best: "Affirmations are how we travel the road from deprived to deserving [9:p.18]." That line was buried among the many pearls of wisdom she imparts in her wonderful book. It struck me as being so emotionally accurate. Many individuals suffering from addictive and compulsive disorders do not feel deserving or entitled to a satisfying bountiful life. Practicing daily affirmations, journaling, mindfulness, and expressing our gratitude for life's many gifts will strengthen and empower us and build our resilience. It will help to give us the clarity to create the meaning so essential to our human experience.

FURTHER INFORMATION

BOOK RECOMMENDATIONS

M. J. Ryan wrote an insightful book *Attitudes of Gratitude: How to Give and Receive Joy Everyday of Your Life* [10]. This little volume is full of information on the healing powers of gratitude. Here are some of the topics that would be useful for anyone but especially those in recovery:

- Gratitude Eradicates Worry [10:p.21]
- Gratitude Draws People To Us [10:p.25]
- Gratitude Is The Antidote To Bitterness and Resentment [10:p.27]
- Attitude Is the Only Disability [10:p.71]
- Practice Wonderment [10:p.115]

Melody Beattie offers much wisdom in her book, *Gratitude: Affirming The Good Things In Life*. Her chapter, "The Process of Acceptance," discusses the five-step process first identified by Elisabeth Kübler-Ross in her work with the terminally ill. Beattie discusses these stages in regard to recovery. The stages are denial, anger, bargaining, depression, and acceptance [9]. This book has stood the test of time, is a very good read, and will help clarify issues you may experience on your journey.

I Want To Change My Life: How To Overcome Anxiety, Depression and Addiction was written by Steven M. Melemis Ph.D., M.D. [11]. This is an excellent book to read, especially if you also suffer from depression or anxiety. Dr. Melemis offers a five-point change plan, which is very compatible with the PDMT Model [12]. Of particular importance is his emphasis on stress management and relaxation. This book will help you combine cognitive therapy with relaxation.

As he states in the book, "Mind-body relaxation and cognitive therapy represent the eastern and western approaches to self-help [11],"

Utilizing both approaches provides a powerful set of recovery tools. I highly recommend this resource. I also endorse the daily use of relaxation techniques as part of the rituals and routines of recovery.

REFERENCE LIST

[1] Alcoholics Anonymous World Services, Inc. (2016 August) *The Twelve Steps of Alcoholics Anonymous* [Online]. Available: http://www.aa.org/assets/en_US/smf-121_en.pdf

[2] Merriam-Webster Dictionary. (2017). *mindfulness* [Online]. Available: https://www.merriam-webster.com/dictionary/mindfulness

[3] R. D. Siegel, PsyD, *The Mindfulness Solution: Everyday Practices For Everyday Problems*. New York, NY: Guilford Publications, Inc. 2010, p. 27.

[4] L.G. DiStefano, LCSW, *The Paradigm Developmental Model of Treatment Group Topics*. San Diego, CA: Montezuma Publishing, 2012.

[5] R. Crane, *Mindfulness-based Cognitive Therapy: Distinctive Features*. New York, NY: Routledge/Taylor & Francis Group, 2009.

[6] E. Scott, MS. (2017, Feb.) *Mindfulness Meditation Techniques for Stress Relief* [Online]. Available:

https://www.verywell.com/mindfulness-meditation-techniques-for-stress-relief-3144772
[7] Oxford University Press: English Oxford Living Dictionaries. (2017). *gratitude* [Online]. Available: https://en.oxforddictionaries.com/definition/gratitude
[8] V. E. Frankl, *Man's Search For Meaning: An Introduction to Logotherapy.* New York, NY: Simon and Schuster, 1959.
[9] M. Beattie. *Gratitude: Affirming the Good Things in Life.* New York, NY: Hazelden Foundation, 1992, p. 18.
[10] M. J. Ryan. *Attitudes of Gratitude: How to Give and Receive Joy Every Day of Your Life.* San Francisco, CA: Conari Press/Red Wheel/Weiser LLC., 1999.
[11] S. M. Melemis, Ph.D. M.D., *I Want to Change My Life: How to Overcome Anxiety, Depression and Addiction.* Toronto, Canada: Modern Therapies, 2010, ch. 14, p. 11.
[12] L.G. DiStefano, LCSW and M. Hohman, Ph.D., *The Paradigm Developmental Model of Treatment: A Clinical Guide for Counselors Working with Substance Abusers and the Chemically Dependent.* San Diego, CA: Montezuma Publishing, 2010.

CHAPTER 12

PUTTING IT ALL TOGETHER
PARADIGM 4; THEME 4
TRANSFORMATION

PARADIGM 4: TRANSFORMATION

This is both the final Paradigm and the last theme of the PDMT model. In the prologue, I discussed transformation and the story of Ray. For individuals fortunate enough to stay the course, this theme represents their best self. Intense feelings of gratitude, abundance, wellbeing, humility, and self-love are often described at this stage [1].

For those that have taken the time and made the effort to address both their relationship with addictive substances and the thinking and behaviors of healthy self-regulation, true change really occurs. Giving back to others is also an important ingredient in maintaining a focus on what has been learned. Ray's story presented in the Prologue is a perfect example of this.

Working through the twelve themes of the model, which are as we have discussed, a secular and cognitive/behavioral interpretation of the Twelve Steps of A.A., is a powerful experience [2]. Anyone, with or without substance-use issues, would benefit immensely from adopting a lifestyle that concentrates on these themes. As the stories in this book demonstrate, individuals have the capacity to change their thinking and modify their behavior. A person exhibits a true integration of these themes once they are incorporated and choices are made on a daily basis to reinforce their meaning. That is when true paradigm change occurs.

PUTTING IT ALL TOGETHER

We have focused intently on each of the paradigm themes and their value to recovery. Now let's take a moment and consider how the themes work together. As I explained, they are developmental. Before you can

12 - PUTTING IT ALL TOGETHER

take responsibility, you need to recognize that a problem exists. Before you become willing to change, you need to discern through self-examination what actions would support your goal of sobriety or moderation and what behaviors and attitudes would be detrimental. Before asking for forgiveness or truly accepting a consequence, you need to assume accountability for your actions. Before you can self-regulate in a consistent and healthy way, you need to determine actions you want to repeat and reinforce, and attitudes you want to strengthen.

As we rely on the themes to guide behavior, we replace or minimize dysfunctional and self-destructive patterns. This is the best protection from the common problem of switching addictions.

Unfortunately, nothing works faster than a chemical or a compulsive behavior to make a person immediately feel better. Individuals are at high risk to turn to another addiction (gambling, compulsive sexual behavior, workaholism) if they don't learn and practice non-self-destructive ways to feel good. Finally, if a personal transformation is going to occur, one needs to apply the principals of all the previous themes consistently. Daily self-regulation and the practice of mindfulness anchor transformation.

A MOMENT WITH HALEY

Sometimes we learn how former clients are doing quite by accident. There's a Starbucks close to my home near Balboa Park in San Diego. This particular store has a lovely tree in front. Interestingly, I have run into a number of former clients near that tree. One day I was standing by the tree sipping a coffee when a former client who had attended our treatment program, Counseling and

Recovery Institute (CRI), over a decade before came rushing up.

She greeted me with a big smile. "Georgi, do you remember me?"

I responded, "Haley of course I do. How are you?"

She reached into her bag and took out her wallet. "I want to show you something, look at this." She handed me her wallet and showed me two pictures of her beautiful young daughters who were three and five years old. She stated, "because of the program and you, my daughters will never know their mother was a drunk!"

Her words were so powerful they brought tears to my eyes. I learned that she continued with her A.A. involvement, and after three years met a wonderful man at work, "a normie" who supports her recovery. They have two children together. Haley went on to say that she understood her children were at risk to become alcoholic, so she knew that someday she would indeed tell them about her struggle with alcoholism, but she was so grateful that they would not experience her as a drunk. Haley was beaming. She had a solid marriage, a job nearby that she loved, and two wonderful kids. As busy as her schedule is, she is also a sponsor to other women in A.A.

It's hard to imagine any news that would have made me happier that day. I often reflect on the children I have never met, but whose parents I have treated. I know their lives are infinitely better because of their parents' sobriety.

MEETING JESSICA

Another chance meeting gave me an opportunity to talk with a client after many years. I had traveled to

12 - PUTTING IT ALL TOGETHER

Toronto, Canada in 2005 for Alcoholics Anonymous' World Convention.

As I previously discussed, I was honored that the organization had invited me as a guest to recognize my contributions to the field of addiction medicine. It is my understanding that every five years at their International World Convention, they invite twenty-one non-alcoholic professionals from countries around the world to acknowledge in such a manner.

The convention was an amazing experience. Meetings in many different languages and a variety of other events packed several days of the conference. There were around 40,000 people at the closing event at Rogers Centre.

Soon after I had arrived in Toronto, I was enjoying dinner with my spouse at a lovely restaurant with a magnificent view. As I gazed out the window I felt a hand on my shoulder. There stood Jessica, a woman I had treated at the hospital in the 1980s.

Jessica greeted me warmly, and proudly showed me a beautiful engagement ring. She planned on getting married in a few months. Despite the fact she was in her mid-40s, Jessica had dated little in the past. We chatted for a few minutes as she caught me up. She was still working as an accountant and had continued on and off with the therapist to whom I had referred her. That therapeutic relationship and her A.A. involvement had endured over 20 years.

The chance meeting with Jessica felt spiritual. Here I was at this extraordinary convention, thinking about so many of the clients I had worked with over my career. I had traveled thousands of miles to be there and there were thousands of people in attendance. Who should I run into but one of the first and most challenging cases I had at the hospital.

When I first met Jessica, she had great difficulty talking about herself and verbalizing her feelings, so much so that she could barely participate in group therapy. She had experienced terrible emotional abuse as a child, and had emerged from that dreadful trauma and turned to alcohol to soothe her feelings of abandonment and mistrust. I knew it would be essential for her to engage in ongoing therapy because of these issues.

At the conclusion of the hospital inpatient treatment, I introduced Jessica to a highly skilled and engaging therapist. They worked together for over 20 years. Jessica credits this therapeutic relationship and A.A. with her long-term success. She grew from a fragile and vulnerable woman who could barely articulate her feelings to a self-confident, sober, and insightful individual.

Jessica is among hundreds of individuals I have seen transformed by the power of recovery. Their changes are real and meaningful. The most important "Collective Wisdom" I can share from these individuals is that "CHANGE IS ABSOLUTELY POSSIBLE."

I have witnessed countless individuals create the type of life they have longed for and never thought possible. I am not saying it is easy. Jessica spent over 20 years addressing the trauma and undoing the dysfunctional patterns she developed in her childhood. Also, life continues to present challenges in the here and now.

As a client once told me, "It is sometimes two steps forward and one step back. However, if you keep at it you will still cross the room."

12 - PUTTING IT ALL TOGETHER

Try it, they are right. Don't be discouraged. Growth doesn't happen in a straight line. Sometimes we step back or need to pause in place. The most important thing is to stay committed.

COFFEE WITH CAROLE

I received a call in March of 2017 from a former client who I had treated in 1998. We met for coffee on the day of her 19th sobriety birthday. She had been a very successful corporate director prior to retirement. Over coffee, she recalled our first meeting 19 years before.

"I called you on Saturday, and you saw me on Monday," Carole recalled. "After the assessment we discussed my situation. You confirmed my suspicions that I was very likely in the early to middle stages of alcoholism. We discussed options. You said, 'If you want privacy and time to work on this you could go to an out-of-town treatment program such as Betty Ford. Or, you could immerse yourself in an outpatient treatment program here in the community. Another option is to try A.A. and individual therapy.' I said, 'A.A. and therapy.'

"The very next day I walked into an A.A. meeting near my home. I entered a large room of a church complex and sat next to a biker with a helmet. I had dressed for work and felt very uncomfortable. The biker looked at me and said, 'Lady, I think you want to go out there to another room.' I nodded my thanks and walked in the direction he was pointing. I found my way to a beautiful library room filled with about a dozen women. It was their Tuesday morning A.A. meeting for women. I have spent virtually every Tuesday morning for the last 19 years in that room."

I asked Carole what was the pull that created such a commitment. She responded with the following "Collective Wisdom": "THERE IS SUCH WISDOM IN THAT A.A. ROOM."

This extraordinarily bright corporate professional found a home group that she could trust and rely on. She frequently went for coffee with the women following their meeting, and the bonds of friendship she developed have lasted and grown through the years. When I asked her what advice she would pass on, she said, "Find a support meeting that you feel comfortable with and make it part of your weekly routine."

Commitment is essential to many endeavors. The time you devote to establishing an active base of support can prove invaluable when you hit the proverbial bump in the road, a difficult patch of time, or a stressful situation. In recovery, it's also helpful to acknowledge your sobriety-based commitments regularly. Create a vision of your sober life. It helps to verbally reinforce the recovery behaviors that hopefully have become routine and support those commitments.

JOHN'S COMMITMENT AND VISION

I recently spoke with a colleague who worked with me at CRI, our former outpatient substance abuse clinic. She reminded me of a client who came to our alumni party to acknowledge the closing of our facility. John made a speech that night, and as the expression goes, there was not a dry eye in the house.

John had come to the clinic five years before in terrible shape. He was holding onto his job by a thread. He was on a last chance agreement with his employer. He was in terrible debt, had lost his beautiful home, and

12 - PUTTING IT ALL TOGETHER

was living in a small studio apartment. He was alone and miserable when we first met. John recognized that drugs were destroying him. He committed himself to a recovery process, where weeks of recovery turned into months and months turned into years.

John made a moving speech that night. He spoke of envisioning the type of man he wanted to be and the kind of life he wanted to lead. He spoke of the gifts of recovery and at the end of the speech he took the precious bundle from his wife's hands and held up his baby boy.

"This is the best gift," he said. "I will continue to work every day to be a good father and husband."

So many years have passed, but I can still see him holding up his baby boy, full of the joy and wisdom that sobriety brings, as if it were yesterday.

There is so much to be hopeful about. Advances in science have given us greater information about the brain and addictive process. More refined medications have become available to assist in the early stages of detoxification and recovery. We have a greater understanding about medication management and the relationship between addiction and mental health disorders such as anxiety, bipolar, depression, and personality disorders. Great strides have been made in understanding the importance of biochemistry and genetics. Information is now available about the role of various nutritional supplements that can enhance and stabilize recovery. New educational opportunities and certification programs have been developed for individuals to become knowledgeable counseling professionals and offer a greater degree of assistance than ever before. Perhaps more importantly, self-help organizations continue to grow and flourish in communities around the world. They offer hope, support, and a real alternative to addiction.

I would be remiss not to reiterate that many people do not enjoy the positive outcomes of John and the other successful clients I have mentioned in this book. They might not have had the resources, coaching, commitment, motivation, or fellowship to create a successful sobriety. Other individuals may have had the resources and exposure, but for a variety of reasons were unable to initiate or sustain a lasting sobriety.

As a therapist, I have learned much from working with these individuals. They have helped identify roadblocks, relapse dynamics, and other important issues that I have been able to pass on and discuss with others. I also recognize that there are scores of individuals who never make it into a self-help group or counseling office. Perhaps one of those individuals will pick up this book and be motivated to initiate a change process and begin a life of sobriety. Perhaps a counseling professional will read this book and consider working through The Paradigm Developmental Model of Treatment themes with their clients. I believe this book might prove useful in the classroom for instruction on this treatment approach.

If one more life can be changed for the better by the collective wisdom shared in this book, then writing this has been a very worthwhile and meaningful endeavor.

Best wishes on your journey.

REFERENCE LIST

[1] L.G. DiStefano, LCSW and M. Hohman, Ph.D., *The Paradigm Developmental Model of Treatment:*

12 - PUTTING IT ALL TOGETHER

A Clinical Guide for Counselors Working with Substance Abusers and the Chemically Dependent. San Diego, CA: Montezuma Publishing, 2010.

[2] Alcoholics Anonymous World Services, Inc. (2016, Aug.). *The Twelve Steps of Alcoholics Anonymous* [Online]. Available: http://www.aa.org/assets/en_US/smf-121_en.pdf

PARADIGM DEVELOPMENTAL MODEL OF TREATMENT

FURTHER INFORMATION FOR CLIENTS IN INDIVIDUAL THERAPY

If you are working with a therapist or counselor in your first years of recovery and would like to utilize the PDMT Model, I suggest the following: Each month focus on a PDMT Theme. Read or reread the chapter in this book pertaining to the theme prior to the session (cognitive homework). Discuss the theme in weekly counseling utilizing the various exercises in the text *Paradigm Developmental Model of Treatment: A Clinical Guide for Counselors Working with Substance Abusers and The Chemically Dependent.* Hopefully, your therapist will have a copy of the PDMT textbook so that materials can be duplicated for you. This textbook is available from Montezuma Press or Amazon. If your therapist or counselor does not have a copy, they may ask you to purchase it. Please be advised, it's a large textbook because it was designed for professionals and treatment institutions to use in their treatment programs, and the materials are allowed to be duplicated for clients. Therefore, one book serves many people.

Once you have the materials, following is a list of topics that often are useful to discuss as you work through the various paradigm themes. Together with your therapist or counselor, select the topics that resonate for you. The exercises can be completed in the session (they generally take ten minutes), or could be done prior to the session and brought in for discussion.

PARADIGM CHANGE

PARADIGM 1: PROBLEM RECOGNITION [1]

THEMES:
1. Problem Recognition
2. Looking Beyond Self
3. Letting Go

EXERCISES THAT COULD BE HELPFUL:
A. Motivators and Goals (PDMT p. 85)
B. Identification of High Risk Behaviors (PDMT p. 89)
C. Consequence History (PDMT p. 98)
D. Looking Forward (PDMT p. 100)
E. Decisional Balance Worksheet (PDMT p. 102)
F. Personal Ruler Worksheet (PDMT p. 106)
G. Reaction to A.A./Other Self-Help Meetings (PDMT p. 108)
H. Identifying Cravings and Urges (PDMT p. 111)
I. Determining Unmanageability (PDMT p. 113)

PARADIGM 2: TAKING RESPONSIBILITY [1]

THEMES:
4. Self-Examination
5. Taking Responsibility
6. Willingness/Preparation (For Change)
7. Action to Change
8. Accountability/Empathy

EXERCISES THAT COULD BE HELPFUL:
A. Self-Examination (PDMT p. 121)
B. What Is My Communication Style (PDMT p. 124)

THE COLLECTIVE WISDOM OF RECOVERY

C. High Risk Behavior Change Plan (PDMT p. 126)
D. What Gets in The Way (PDMT p. 128)
E. Revisiting My Goals and Motivators (PDMT p. 130)
F. My Cultural Influences (PDMT p. 132)
G. Reducing Negative Impact (PDMT p. 133)
H. Positive Impact (PDMT p. 134)
I. Urge Monitoring Card (PDMT p. 137)
J. Trigger Response Plan (PDMT p. 138)
K. Checklist of Social Pressure Situations (PDMT p. 140)
L. Identifying Social Pressures (PDMT p. 141)
M. Situations and Coping Responses (PDMT p. 142)
N. Learning From Collective Wisdom (PDMT p. 144)
O. Old/New Behaviors (PDMT p.1 46)
P. What Is in My Control (PDMT p. 148)

PARADIGM 3: SELF-REGULATION AND
PARADIGM 4: TRANSFORMATION [1]

THEMES:
9. Asking Forgiveness: Accepting Consequences
10. Self-Regulation
11. Mindfulness
12. Transformation/Giving Back

EXERCISES THAT COULD BE HELPFUL:
A. How I Have Changed (PDMT p. 158)
B. Growth Zone Worksheet (PDMT p. 160)
C. Unknown Zone Worksheet (PDMT p. 161)

PARADIGM CHANGE

- D. Self-Regulation Planning (PDMT pp. 163-165)
- E. Amends (PDMT p. 167)
- F. ACA: Old Behaviors Today (PDMT pp. 169-170)
- G. Building My Future (PDMT p. 172)
- H. Action Plan (PDMT p. 184)

ABOUT THE AUTHOR

L. Georgi DiStefano is a licensed clinical social worker with extensive experience in the clinical management of substance abuse/chemical dependency treatment programs and employee assistance services. She is a popular speaker on the Paradigm Developmental Model of Treatment and workplace conflict resolution and has written extensively on both topics.

She recently retired as the Executive/Clinical Director of the San Diego State University Center for Alcohol and Drug Studies and Services, Driving Under the Influence (DUI) Program. For 14 years she managed a multi-million-dollar budget with over 3,000 active weekly clients and a staff of 85 people.

She previously managed the Employee Assistance Program (EAP) for Kaiser Permanente Hospital System in San Diego, California.

In the 1980s and 1990s, she was the Director of the Alcohol and Substance Abuse Program at Mesa Vista Hospital and the Founder and Executive Director of the Counseling and Recovery Institute in San Diego, California.

Ms. DiStefano has been an adjunct assistant professor at San Diego State University in the School of Social Work, College of Health and Human Services for over 15 years.

She is the lead author of the book and method, *Paradigm Developmental Model of Treatment: A Clinical Guide for Counselors Working with Substance Abusers and the Chemically Dependent*, which has been translated into several languages. She also wrote *The Paradigm Developmental Model of Treatment: Group Topics,* which has been utilized widely in substance abuse treatment and DUI programs. She is co-author of the award-winning book, *It's All Your Fault at Work* with William Eddy, LCSW, Esq.

In 1990, Ms. DiStefano was awarded the Clinical Social Worker of the Year from the Clinical Society of Social Work and National Association of Social Workers (NASW), California Chapter. In 2011, she received the National Association of Social Workers Lifetime Achievement Award, also from NASW, California Chapter.

She has spoken nationally and internationally on both the Paradigm Treatment Model and Managing High Conflict Personalities, giving frequent seminars in locations such as Japan, Canada, Greece, New York, Chicago, New Mexico, Paraguay, and Buenos Aires. She also provides management consultation and executive coaching, in addition to her private practice and seminar work.

In 2014, she was recognized for her significant contributions to the social work profession by being inducted into the California Social Work Hall of Distinction.

BOOKS BY L. GEORGI DISTEFANO, LCSW

- *Paradigm Developmental Model of Treatment: A Clinical Guide for Counselors Working with Substance Abusers and the Chemically Dependent.*
  L. Georgi DiStefano, LCSW and Melinda Hohman, Ph.D.
- *Paradigm Developmental Model of Treatment Group Topics.*
  L. Georgi DiStefano, LCSW.
- *It's All Your Fault at Work: Managing Narcissists and Other High Conflict People.*
  Bill Eddy, LCSW, Esq. and L. Georgi DiStefano, LCSW.
- *New Ways for Work: Personal Skills for Productive Relationships: Coaching Manual.*
  Bill Eddy, LCSW, Esq. and L. Georgi DiStefano, LCSW.
- *New Ways for Work: Personal Skills for Productive Relationships: Workbook.*
  Bill Eddy, LCSW, Esq. and L. Georgi DiStefano, LCSW.

PARADIGM CHANGE

www.ingramcontent.com/pod-product-compliance
Lightning Source LLC
Chambersburg PA
CBHW041310240426
43661CB00064B/2885